WALKING THE LINE

WALKING THE LINE

Scenes from an Army Childhood

Kevin T. Brophy

MAINSTREAM
PUBLISHING

EDINBURGH AND LONDON

ACKNOWLEDGMENTS

Some of the illustrations in this book come courtesy of Galway archivist, Tom Kenny, and of Col Dave Taylor and his staff at the embryonic museum in the Barracks: the author and publisher wish to record their sincere gratitude to them all.

First published in Great Britain in 1994 by
MAINSTREAM PUBLISHING COMPANY (EDINBURGH) LTD
7 Albany Street
Edinburgh EH1 3UG

ISBN 1 85158 638 5

The publisher gratefully acknowledges the financial assistance of The Scottish Arts Council in the production of this book

A catalogue record for this book is available from the British Library

Typeset in Garamond by CentraCet Limited, Cambridge
Printed and bound in Great Britain by
Butler & Tanner Ltd, Frome and London

DEDICATION

For Raymond Forde and Alphonsus Cleere
who nurtured a patrician flame

AUTHOR'S NOTE

This book is written only with love: I have, nevertheless, changed most of the names of family and neighbours – they are entitled to their privacy, and their memories are no less precious to them than mine are to me.

ONE

Through the green iron railings of the veranda I could see the Square, where my father and the other soldiers went on parade every morning. Even from this height on the upper floor of the Quarters, you couldn't see the entire Square: only a strip of it was visible through the gap between the canteen and the NCOs' Mess on the left and the Stores on the right. What was stored in the Stores I hadn't yet figured out: sometimes I'd see soldiers going into or coming out of the Stores, but what exactly they or anybody else did inside the grey stone building opposite the Quarters remained a mystery.

Sometimes I'd play a private game on the veranda of the Married Quarters. I'd begin in the spot I now occupied, outside the entrance to Number 20, and I'd move to the left and right, testing how the view of the Square narrowed between the buildings opposite until finally the parade ground was blocked completely from view. You could see a section of the Square over the roof of the Stores, even when you moved as far right as the wider area of the veranda, above the Arch but, in my personal game, you could count only what was visible between the Stores and the NCOs' Mess.

The railings along the veranda were vertical, topped by two horizontal bars, and with a single horizontal bar running along the bottom. The vertical bars were square; the horizontal bars were wider and flat. You could fit your boots between the upright bars and stand on the bottom rail, so that you could see even further.

This morning you could see for miles, out beyond the perimeter walls of the Barracks, across the playing-fields and the bay as far as the snow-capped hills on the other side of the water. The November day had the sharpness of knives and the wind, blowing in from the bay, pierced your skin like Apache arrows. I drew my olive-green

7

balaclava closer around my face and then tried to shuck the sleeves of my coat further down around my hands so that I did not feel the touch of the cold veranda railing against my fingers.

A thin skin of unthawed ice rimed the railings. Snow blanketed the Square and clung to the roofs of the Stores and the other buildings. Although there had been no parade that morning, the white snow on the Square was pocked and churned by the soldiers' boots.

'No parade this morning,' my father had said, pulling the net curtain of the kitchen window to one side, but he went on polishing the brass buttons of his tunic and his overcoat. You had to Brasso your buttons whether there was a parade or not: you polished them until they gleamed like gold, trapped like bulging metal eyes in the slit of your button-stick.

Sometimes I'd watch from the veranda as the ritual of morning parade unfolded on the Square: the lined ranks of the soldiers, the officer facing them, the sergeant who enacted some special role in the liturgy, marching between officer and men, barking commands in Irish that carried unintelligibly up to my spot outside Number 20.

Number 20 was where we lived – my parents, my sister Miriam, my brother Jacky, the baby Danny, and myself. The Quarters were where Mammies and Daddies lived with their children. Billets like A-Block and B-Block, on the far side of the Square, were where the soldiers slept; soldiers didn't live anywhere, but they slept in the billets.

It was strange, how a *billet* sounded like a *bullet*, but one was for killing Indians in the Wild West and the other was just for soldiers to sleep in. Once I'd sneaked into A-Block with Tommy, crept up the stone staircase and peered through the gap in the half-open door at the rows of narrow beds along the wall, but then a shirt-sleeved soldier, lounging on his bunk, had roared something at us and we'd fled in panic, back down the steps and out of A-Block. Kit Carson had never ridden as hard to escape a bunch of blood-thirsty Pawnees as we rode our tiring mounts across the Square to the sanctuary of the Quarters. We hadn't drawn breath till we'd reined in at the Arch and there, breathless, we swore each other to secrecy; discovery of our escapade might bring not only hard words from our Dads, but also a clip on the ear.

My father had given me a penny that morning. I pushed my hand under my overcoat and into my trouser pocket to finger the coin. The metal was warm in the small cocoon of my pocket. I didn't need to take it out to know that it was an Irish penny, with a hen on the front and a harp on the back, dated 1943, the year I was born. I liked our own Irish pennies better than the English ones, with their heads of English kings on the front and the peculiar sitting warrior on the back. My penny was shining from the polishing I'd given it with Brasso. It seemed a pity to spend it, but you had to spend it if you wanted to have a penny bar. You couldn't keep your penny and still have a penny bar to chew.

The penny was a gift for this special day, my first day at school.

I'd been pestering my mother for weeks and weeks to let me go to school. Unrelentingly I had beaten down all her defences. Hadn't I often walked The Line into town with her and why wouldn't I be able to walk it every day into school? And, yes, Tommy and Bobby had older brothers to go to school with, but neither Art nor Paul had an older brother, and they went to school, so why couldn't I? And anyway I had no one to play with until the other lads arrived back in the Barracks after school every afternoon . . .

Mammy had never denied me anything for as long as she denied me the gift of school.

Her defences had crumbled in the end, worn down by my tears and sulky assaults. Her objections, resolute for so long, had finally disappeared with the sudden unexpectedness of the carpet of white snow sliding irrevocably down the purple-slated roof of the Stores. One moment the snow was there, opposite you, a white, creamy tea-cosy snug against the chimneys, and the next moment it was crashing to the ground in a flurry of icy spray.

'All right,' Mammy had said the night before, 'you can go to school.'

'When?' I'd asked when I had grasped the enormity of her capitulation. 'When, Mammy?'

'In the morning – tomorrow morning.'

The immediacy of it was something frightening. Now that the dream I had chased so passionately for so long was within my grasp, I would have welcomed a few days' respite before I finally held it in my hands.

Now it was Mammy's turn to be relentless. Now that she had

yielded her position, it was as if she could no longer bear to see the ruins of her breached redoubt.

'Tomorrow,' she'd said again. 'In the morning.'

And so I stood on the veranda, surveying the white stillness of the Barracks, waiting for Mammy to come out from Number 20 to take me to school. It seemed that the whole Barracks was waiting for her, wrapped in its greatcoat of crystal whiteness, the snow-fringed grey lorries ranged immobile and silent along the edge of the Square.

The sound of the door of Number 20 opening and closing rattled against the hard-edged silence. I heard her footsteps on the stone floor of the hall we shared with Number 19, where the Hayeses lived, and when I turned around from the railings I saw Mammy pulling the outside door of the hall shut behind her. She was wearing her best scarf, the big one with the Lourdes and Fatima chapels on it. A wave of her black hair pushed out under the front of the scarf, like a soft cloud hanging upside down under a church steeple of her scarf. Her forehead eased itself out of its habitual frown when she looked at me, and her wide straight mouth softened into a smile. 'Are you frozen standing out here?'

She didn't wait for my answer but took my hands in hers and began rubbing them vigorously. The good red shopping-bag swung by its strap from her left wrist as she worked her hands back and forth over my palms and knuckles. I could smell the sweet smell of the yellow stuff from the small bottle that she dabbed behind her ears on special days.

'I wish to God I'd learned how to knit gloves,' she said, more to herself than to me. 'I never did manage to get the hang of the same gloves or even a pair of oul' socks.'

'I'm not cold,' I said.

She knitted jumpers for us all. The needles would click with effortless speed all through the evening after tea while she sat beside the range until it was bedtime. When she bought new wool on Fridays I'd have to hold the hanks stretched across my pillared palms until she had wound the wool into a ball. When I'd asked her once why they didn't make wool in balls, she'd laughed at me and said: 'Sure how could they make it in a ball? Doesn't the wool always come in a hank!' And she'd gone on winding the red wool into a soft and growing ball.

'All the same,' she said to me, 'it'd be nice to have a pair of gloves to keep your hands warm.'

'They'd only get drenched wet makin' snowballs and sure then they couldn't keep your hands warm.'

She ceased her rubbing and bent her head close to me until our foreheads touched. Through the woollen balaclava I could feel the warmth of her hands on the nape of my neck. 'Always an answer,' she said to me, and her breath was warm upon my face. 'It really is time you were going to school.'

'Can we go now, Mammy?' I asked. Art and Tommy and the others were long gone, but Mammy had said we shouldn't arrive too early on my first day. 'If we don't go soon, Mammy, the school will be finished for the day!'

Her forehead creased once more into its frown and there was a sadness of resignation in the way she shook her head. 'Ye're all in such a hurry to grow up, and God only knows what hurry is on ye at all.' The momentary sadness passed, a black cloud scudding across the face of the bright sun, and then she smiled again. 'Now,' she said briskly, 'I want you to wear your new pixie for your first day at school.'

'But, Mammy—'

'No "buts",' she said, and her tone of voice made it clear that she would brook no negotiations on this issue. With one smooth movement she drew the dark-green balaclava off my head and dropped it into her shopping-bag. For an instant her fingers played with my hair, dark as her own, smoothing it down, and then her hand reached into the shopping-bag.

I looked with misgiving at the fawn-coloured pixie, with the matching woollen strap that buttoned across under your chin. She fixed the woollen pixie on my head and pulled it more snugly around my ears. I flinched as she tried to draw the strap under my chin to meet the button. 'But, Mammy—'

'You're not going into school for your first day with an army balaclava on your head,' she interrupted. 'What would the teacher think of us at all?'

And what would the other boys think if they saw me with a pixie on my head? A balaclava was for men; the soldiers wore them under their helmets, their faces blackened with polish and burnt cork, when they were doing manoeuvres in the bushes around the sports fields.

'Now, doesn't that feel nice and warm!'

I couldn't tell her that the balaclava was warmer. She'd knitted the headgear herself, checking periodically to make sure that it fitted correctly. Sometimes you'd see another boy wearing a new jumper that was too tight or too loose, or the sleeves were too short or too long, and you'd be glad that your mother was the best knitter in the whole Married Quarters.

She kissed me and I smiled at her.

'It's nice, Mammy,' I said. I'd have to remember to whip the pixie off my head very quickly, just as we reached the school, when she wouldn't notice. Sometimes you had to be extra careful with Mammies and Daddies, so that you didn't hurt their feelings.

I let her take my hand in hers and we moved briskly along the veranda towards the Arch. The Arch was both the physical and social centre of the Quarters. It housed the two flights of stone steps that led up to the veranda, and its wide, arched space at ground-level provided a natural meeting-place for both women and children. Two families lived in the Quarters on the upper floor of the Arch, one on either side of the staircase, but the home on the Arch's ground floor was a double quarters, and was the sole preserve of Bobby Dunne's family.

The steps of the Arch rang under the studs of my black boots. The studs came on a blue card that Mammy bought in town. She got the loan of a last from the Barracks shoemaker and hammered the studs into the soles of the boots. There were two special crescent-shaped tips that fitted neatly around the toes of the boots. All the boys in the Barracks had studs in their boots. The studs made the soles last longer and they were better for sliding on the ice. I was proud of the noise they made on the steps of the Arch.

'Good mornin', Mrs Brophy.'

'Good mornin', Mrs Dunne,' Mammy answered.

Mrs Dunne was standing with her arms folded at the entrance to the Arch. It sometimes seemed to me that Mrs Dunne never left this spot, but was permanently rooted there on the stone step, wrapped in her blue smock, eternally observing the comings and goings of Barracks life. I'd heard Big Paddy once say that Major Timoney had to get Mrs Dunne's permission before he could change any of the rules of the Barracks. Big Paddy was thirteen and wore long trousers, but I didn't believe him anyway.

'Ye're taking him in for his first day at school?'

Mrs Dunne knew everything. Maybe it was because she was so much older than Mammy, with lank grey hair. Mr Dunne was the Barracks tailor. He wore brown-rimmed glasses and was bald. He spoke to me sometimes when I was in the Dunnes' kitchen, swapping comics or playing ludo with Bobby, and you had to strain to hear what he was saying in his quiet voice, soft as the cloth he worked with on the big foot-pedal sewing-machine.

'What age is he now?' Mrs Dunne asked.

You didn't have to strain at all to hear what Mrs Dunne was saying.

I pulled impatiently at my mother's hand but she drew back so that we stood beside Mrs Dunne. It wasn't good manners, she told me later, to walk away when somebody was speaking to you, not even if it was your first day at school. (She got very cross when I suggested that, in that case, good manners were just silly.)

'He's five,' Mammy answered.

I pulled fiercely at Mammy's coat.

'He's tall for his age, God bless him,' Mrs Dunne said.

I went on pulling at the skirt of Mammy's coat.

'Sure he's healthy anyway, thank God,' Mammy said. This time I almost unbalanced her, so fiercely did I pull at her coat. She looked down at me, frowning. 'What is it?' she asked me, and there was a hint of impatience in her tone.

'I'm not five anymore,' I said, 'I'm five and a half.'

My mother laughed.

Mrs Dunne smiled.

'Well, I am!' I insisted. It wasn't a bit funny. 'It's after the seventeenth now, so I'm not five anymore. I'm five and a half.' I'd worked it out carefully, and it didn't seem to me to be a smiling matter to claim that I was still only five. My insistence seemed only to deepen the women's amusement.

'He's like the rest of them,' Mrs Dunne said, and for the life of me I couldn't figure out what she meant.

Her breath hung beside her face in the frosty air. It reminded me of gunsmoke from Kit Carson's pistol after he'd picked off another thievin' redskin.

'We'd better be going,' Mammy said, 'or we'll be meeting the other lads coming home on the Line.'

I moved down off the step, eager to be going.

'All the same,' Mrs Dunne said, 'isn't he a bit old for startin'? All the other lads are only the same age and they're at school this long while.'

Her words shamed me. I had been making the same protestations to Mammy for months past. I felt my ears burning and I tried to pull Mammy along with me by the hand. Her grip tightened on my hand, however, and I was forced to stop.

'He's time enough for startin',' Mammy said, and I recognised again that tone of conviction that would not be shaken. 'Anyway,' my mother added, 'he won't be at any loss – he's able to add and subtract, and he can read and say all his prayers.'

'And I can tell the time on the clock,' I added.

'And he can tell the time on the clock,' Mammy repeated.

When I looked up at her I could see the way her face had broken into a broad smile.

'And I'm going to the Brothers,' I added defiantly. The other lads were in High Babies at the nuns' school in town.

'We'll be off so,' Mammy said. 'Good day to you now, Mrs Dunne.'

There was an extra lift in her step as we walked away. I had to hurry to keep up with her. We passed Number 4, where Small Paddy McDonagh lived – Big Paddy McDonagh, who was my pal Tommy's older brother, lived in Number 6, on the other side of the Arch, but they were different McDonaghs, and I had found it confusing when we'd first moved into the Quarters. On past Number 3 we went, and past Number 2, and then up the steps that separated the Married Quarters territory from the rest of the Barracks.

Mick Sheehan, the armourer, waved to us from behind the half-door of the armourer's shop. The armourer was the fellow who fixed soldiers' rifles and made sure that they fired properly.

'Are ye off to make a scholar of him?' Mick called out to us. He was a small man with a fox-like face. He was wearing his tunic this morning: in the summertime, when he wore only his army vest, the blue-veined muscles on his short arms surprised you, and you sensed the strength that handled with ease not only rifles but the heavy barrels of the machine-guns, and the metal entrails of tanks and trucks that covered the benches of his shop.

Mammy waved back to him. 'We have to start anyway,' she said, cheerily.

'Make a general out of him,' Mick shouted, 'and then he can promote me out of this oul' shop.'

Mammy laughed. I was glad we didn't stop to talk more. In a moment we had drawn away from the armourer's shop in the bottom corner of the Magazine. The Gate of the Barracks lay just ahead of us.

'Mammy?'

'What is it?' she asked me.

'Could I be a general?' There was no general in the barracks, but I had seen generals in my comics.

Mammy stopped and looked earnestly at me. 'Of course you could be a general,' she said to me. 'You can be anything you like in the whole world.'

'How can you be a general if your Daddy isn't an officer?'

She laughed, the gurgling laugh that I loved, from deep down in her throat. 'Musha, God help your head,' she said to me. 'Sure what has that got to do with anything! You can be anything you want to be, it doesn't matter what your Daddy is or isn't. Don't you understand that?'

I nodded. 'Okay.' I said.

All the same, I wasn't sure. A general could give orders to anybody, and how could I be giving orders to my own Daddy? I kept my doubts to myself, and we hurried on across the snow towards the Gate.

The Gate wasn't the same as the gates. The great metal-barred gates, tall as the Barracks walls, were opened by the red-capped PA to allow lorries and other vehicles in or out of the Barracks.

If you were on foot, or if you had a bicycle, you went through the Gate. The Gate was a tiny, two-roomed building that straddled the Barracks wall, next to the main gates. It was presided over by a military policeman or PA, as he was known. (Years later I would learn that 'military policeman' became PA, the abbreviation for the Irish language term, *póilín airm*.)

You entered the Gate from inside the Barracks by an ordinary door with a brass knob. Not even the pot-bellied stove inside could quite remove the chill from the stone-floored Gate. Big Bartley was warming his hands beside the stove when Mammy and I entered.

'It's a hoor opening and closing them gates all day,' he said cheerfully. 'They're so cold you'd think your fingers'd stick to them.'

'It's hardy right enough,' Mammy said.

'Hardy isn't the word for it,' Bartley said. 'The wireless says there's more snow promised for tonight, God knows where it's all coming from.' He was thoughtful for a moment, but then his round red face expanded into a grin. 'Sure more snow might keep the bloody trucks off the road anyway, and save us running in and out to those so-and-so gates all day.'

Mammy laughed. 'Sure things could always be worse,' she said.

I stamped my studded boots on the stone floor, wondering why grown-ups could never pass one another without exchanging inanities about the weather.

'Your young man is getting impatient,' Bartley said, glancing at me.

'It's his first day at school,' my mother told him.

'It's all before him,' Bartley said. He still made no move from the pot-bellied stove.

'We should be getting on,' Mammy said, 'or we'll be meeting ourselves coming back.'

The PA moved at last, rubbing his palms together as he crossed the small office towards the outside door. This outside door of the Gate was made of thick wood, reinforced with metal. It had a small window at head-height through which the PA could inspect anybody trying to get into the Barracks.

Bartley drew back the great iron bolt that fastened the heavy door. The door swung open easily on well-oiled hinges. The icy wind hit us, twirling and twisting around the open door into the Gate.

'Good luck so,' Mammy said, taking my hand and drawing me close to her.

'Good luck with the schoolin',' Bartley shouted.

The great door of the Gate slammed shut behind us. We were outside the Barracks. Ahead lay the Line.

I had walked the Line a few times previously, always with my mother, but never when it was covered thickly with snow. You could see it curving in front like a white band of ribbon that tied the Barracks to the town.

Only in the distance was it truly white. Underfoot, the snow was flattened into brackish footprints by the boots of those who had gone before us. Here and there the snow was packed down into hard snake-tracks by the tyres of bicycles: their tracks were edged by low ridges of discoloured, icy snow.

I wanted to climb inside the wire fence to get the white, creamy snow that lay on the sleepers of the railway tracks, but Mammy objected. It was dangerous, she said, and besides, wasn't I in a hurry to get to school?

We hurried on, our heads bent into the icy wind that cut into our faces and whistled in the telegraph wires over our heads. We left the first downward hill behind us, and the small army chapel, thatched now with whitest snow; we padded across Paddy Walsh's bridge, and I looked down, but you couldn't see the cross of stones on the grass below, because the field was thickly carpeted with snow. The blackness of the mounds of coal waste that the railway workers tipped out onto the embankment beside the bridge was hidden beneath the all-enveloping whiteness. Nothing stirred in the silent white landscape of the Furze, the whine-covered marshlands that stretched away below us on either side of the Line. In the near distance the wind whipped the sea onto the rocky shore.

We hardly spoke on the stretch between Paddy Walsh's bridge and the middle bridge. Our silence grew, not out of the intense cold and the effort of our hurried walking, but out of our joined hands, our togetherness on this frozen pathway between home and school. I looked back once and felt a stab in my heart for the white wonder of the Barracks on the hill, like a silver galleon commanding an icy sea, its green, white and gold flag stiffened by the wind on top of the Magazine.

I hadn't realised I was standing still until Mammy shook my hand and said to me: 'It's lovely, isn't it?'

I drew my eyes from the Barracks and I met her glance and I tried to say something, but no words would come. She bent towards me and her lips felt warm on my forehead.

I was conscious of a secret moment shared only by Mammy and myself, although I would have been unable to describe whatever it was that we had shared. It included the snow-whitened Barracks, and the wind in the telegraph wires, and her unexpected kiss, but it encompassed something more also, and it was that elusive extra that I could not define.

Across the middle bridge we padded, and soon the boards of Lough Atalia bridge were drumming under our feet. This was the longest and the last bridge – you didn't count the small bridge at the top of the Bandroom Hill. The open mouth of the railway station loomed cavernously ahead, blackness rimmed by a white-lipped hemisphere.

You felt that the journey was over once you stood on top of the Bandroom Hill. The town lay below, the grey bulk of the station on the left, the snowy expanse of the Square in front, with the black perimeter railings turned to white candles by the snow.

'Nearly there,' Mammy said. 'You'll be in school soon.'

You had to be more careful of your footing when you stepped off the Line onto the tarred surface of the road outside the station. Here the snow had been churned by turning buses into a slushy mess that had itself begun to freeze over. Our progress downhill past the station entrance was slow and deliberate, but it was easier on the pavement around the corner, in front of the station hotel, for the hotel staff had cleared the pavement of snow: it was piled up like a filthy rampart along the side of the road.

We made better progress, too, on the incline up the square: here too the footpath was cleared of snow. The square itself was a two-tier tablecloth of white: there was no hint in the still air of the excited shouts and yelps that had been flung from the chairoplanes and swinging-boats last summer, when Mammy had taken me in one evening to Tofts. For all its changing, this town square would never be like our own Square in the Barracks, where the soldiers went on parade . . .

The town was quiet under its coat of snow. The doors of the shops were firmly shut against the cold, but their windows were full of things that you could buy if you had loads of money. In Shop Street the windows of the jeweller's shop were bright with rings and bracelets and watches, but it was the clock above the window that I wanted to see. I drew Mammy quickly along until we stood outside Glynn's toyshop and could read the big clock high up on the wall of the jeweller's shop.

'It's ten to eleven, Mammy,' I said. I waited for her praise: she had taught me to read the time just the week before on the alarm clock that stood on the mantelpiece.

'You're a great boy,' she said, and I grew taller under her words.

The words DUBLIN TIME stood out in big letters on the wall, under the clock.

'What's "Dublin Time", Mammy?'

'You'll be the death of me with all your questions!'

'But what is it, Mammy?' I persisted. 'Why does it have "Dublin Time" under the clock?'

'Just to let you know that it's the same time in Dublin as it is here,' Mammy said.

The general in charge of the whole army lived in a huge barracks in Dublin. Dublin was the capital of Ireland, so the general had to live there.

'Can we go on now?' Mammy was smiling down at me.

'Is it the same time everywhere in the world, Mammy?'

'Sure why wouldn't it be the same time,' Mammy said. 'What other time would it be?'

A small black car ploughed its slow passage through the slush of Shop Street towards the square. It made me dizzy to think of the whole world, and it was ten to eleven everywhere.

'Don't worry your head about it,' Mammy said. 'All you have to think about is that it's ten to eleven at home.'

It was funny how she always seemed to know what I was thinking. There was a story about a mind-reader in a comic, but he had a black cape and a tall hat, and Mammy just lived in the Barracks at Number 20.

'We'll be frozen to the ground if we stand here much longer,' Mammy said.

'It's eight minutes to eleven now,' I said, as I watched the big hand make a jerky jump upwards.

'C'mon,' Mammy said, 'or we'll never get you started at school!'

'Why don't you say "eight to eleven" like "ten to eleven"?'

'Questions, always questions!'

'But why, Mammy, why?'

'Because that's the why!'

I was silent. 'Because that's the why' wasn't an answer at all; it was what you said when you didn't want to be bothered giving an answer. I pretended to look at the toys in Glynn's window: soon they'd be putting all the Christmas things on display, the guns and dolls and dolls'-houses. I kept my hands in my pockets going down the street. At the Four Corners we had to turn right.

Mammy held me by the shoulder but there was no traffic on the road.

On the other footpath Mammy stopped and stooped over me. 'I don't know why we don't say "eight to eleven" like we say "ten to eleven" and "five to eleven"', she said to me. 'It's just the way we tell the time, that's all.'

I felt sorry now for having been sulky coming down the street. She smelled lovely in the cold morning. 'It's probably just like five-ten-fifteen-twenty,' I said magnanimously.

'I expect it is,' Mammy said, fixing my pixie again. 'Now we really *have* to go on!'

'Forward ho!' I said seriously. Sometimes Kit Carson called out that command as he waved the wagon-train onward.

My mother laughed but said nothing. Up the narrow street we went, past Monaghan's sweetshop and the pork butchers with the strings of sausages in the window, and then left into the street which housed the school. You couldn't see the school from the road. You turned right into a narrow lane beside the big house with the silver railings, a lane so narrow that you'd think it was leading nowhere.

It did lead somewhere – into a great open quadrangle, laid out in quartered lawns, now covered by snow, and surrounded by tall, imposing buildings that had grown grand with a rich covering of ivy. There were tall windows glinting in the white glare, taller than any I had seen in the Barracks, and the doorway in the corner of the quadrangle was bigger and wider than the entrance of the Gate.

At the mouth of the lane I stopped. I felt dwarfed by these buildings, these windows, that wide doorway. I moved closer to the shelter of my mother's overcoat.

I felt the pressure of her hand on mine. 'It's all right, *a ghrá*,' she said to me. 'The monk knows you're coming in – I called in to see him yesterday.'

'The monk?'

'Brother Matthew, the teacher in charge of the infants' class.'

'Honest to God?'

'Honest to God.'

From the school across the white lawns, came the sound of chanting. The chanting was in Irish, like the soldiers' commands on parade on the Square.

'But it's all right if you don't want to go,' Mammy was saying. 'You can start after Christmas if you like.'

There'd be no facing Bartley at the Gate if I backed out, or Mrs Dunne at the Arch. And could I ever admit such cowardice to Tommy and Bobby and the other lads in the Barracks? And the chanting sounded familiar and comforting.

I shook my head. 'Let's go, Mammy,' I said.

Our feet crunched on the frozen snow as we headed for the school door. I whipped off the woollen pixie as we went into the tiled porch and stuffed it into my pocket. I was congratulating myself on having done the job without being noticed when I felt my mother's fingers in my hair.

We could hear a deep male voice coming from inside the heavy, varnished door of the classroom.

'You can wear your balaclava tomorrow,' Mammy said to me as she knocked on the door.

I didn't get the chance to answer. The door swung open and Brother Matthew stood there, looking at us.

An hour later I was sitting in the front desk with my arms folded, wishing there was something to do.

'Can you not manage the sums?' Brother Matthew asked, bending over the desk that I shared with two other boys. The loose folds of his happy face were arranged into an expression of sympathy.

I looked up at him with some astonishment. 'I have them done,' I said to him, pointing at the slate on my desk.

Brother Matthew smiled at me. 'Sure maybe you think you have,' he said, 'but we'll take a look anyway.' He turned the slate on the desk so that he could read it. I could hear the boy beside me making scratching noises with his piece of chalk on his blackboard, while the third lad in the desk was making puttering noises with his lips, as if he were saying his prayers.

After a few moments Brother Matthew straightened from his bent position and looked at me quizzically. 'You have them done all right,' he said, 'and they're all right too. Where did you learn the oul' sums?'

'Mammy showed me,' I said.

'Well, she did a right job anyway,' Brother said.

I had liked Brother Matthew from the moment he opened the

21

door to Mammy and myself. He greeted my mother effusively, showed me where to hang my coat with the other drenched overcoats on the wall of the classroom, written my name in Irish in the great register on his table, assured Mammy I'd be all right, and ushered her to the door with more smiles. The entire operation had taken no more than ten minutes. For one brief moment I'd been terrified that my mother was going to kiss me in front of everybody, but she'd merely given me a little wave and then I was alone in my place in the crowded front desk where, Brother Matthew had assured Mammy, he would keep a special eye on me for my first day.

'What's four and two?' he asked me suddenly.

'Six.'

'And three and five?'

'Eight.'

The Brother shook his head.

'You can do your sums to be sure,' he said, almost sadly.

I was beginning to wonder about Brother Matthew. These sums were baby stuff: what was there to be surprised about?

'And I suppose you're able to write your name as well?'

'Yes,' I said.

'Yes, *Brother*,' he said, with an emphasis.

I blushed. 'Yes, Brother.'

He pushed the blackboard towards me and handed me his own stick of white chalk from its perch on top of his ear. 'I can't do joined-up writing,' I said, 'only blocks.'

Brother Matthew waved me on. He perched himself on the edge of the desk, with his feet on the seat, so that I was pushed up against the other two lads while I wrote. His long black gown, down to his shoes, was stretched over his knees like a girl's frock; you could smell the chalk and the cigarettes from it. It was a pleasant, warm smell, mingling with the smell of polish from his shining black shoes and the smell of all the wet coats steaming against the wall.

I felt his eyes upon me as I wrote my name carefully across the bottom of the blackboard: KEVIN T BROPHY.

'What's the "T" for?' Brother Matthew asked, smiling.

'It's for Thomas, my middle name,' I told him, seriously.

The Brother seemed to be trying to hold laughter in, although I could see nothing to laugh at. 'Good man,' Brother Matthew said. He clamped his lips together as if he were in pain. 'Good man,' he said again, climbing down from the top of the desk. I could hear him laughing to himself as he walked back to his own table beside the big blackboard. His heavy frame seemed to shake; when he turned to face the class he was blowing his nose into an enormous white handkerchief but you could see his small eyes dancing like dark coins above the handkerchief. He looked directly at me, and then he winked. Brother Matthew, I decided, was okay, despite some apparent idiosyncrasies.

A little while later he announced that we'd have to eat our lunches indoors, because it had started to snow again. A brief chaos followed, as over fifty boys sought to recover, all at once, their wrapped sandwiches and small bottles of milk from the pockets of coats hanging on the classroom wall. Confusion gave way to contentment as we tucked into our bread and butter and slices of cake: it was my first packed lunch and the sense of occasion lent spice to my hunger.

I took out my penny to admire it while I was eating.

'God, that's a fierce shiny penny,' the boy beside me said. He was a small fellow called Peter. 'It must be a real new penny, is it?'

'It's not new,' I said. I studied my neighbour carefully before deciding that he could be trusted. I held the penny out towards him. 'You can look at the date yourself.'

He took the penny and turned it over in his hand. 'You'd think it was gold,' Peter said.

'I shined it with Brasso,' I told him.

'What's Brasso?'

'It's for shining the buttons on your tunic.'

Peter looked at me blankly.

'You have to shine your buttons when you're going on parade.'

'What parade?'

'Every morning,' I said impatiently, 'When the soldiers go on parade in the Barracks.'

The blankness lingered on Peter's face. 'I don't know where the Barracks is,' he said at last.

'You go out the Line,' I said. I did my best to explain it all to him, but I couldn't be sure of how much he was able to grasp. While I talked, part of me wondered at the strangeness of it all, how some boys didn't even know where the Line was or what a button-stick was for . . .

There would be plenty to tell the lads in the Quarters about my first day at the Brothers, plenty to mull over on the long walk home along the Line to the Barracks.

TWO

When you turned towards the Barracks from the top of the Line you could see the PA seated behind the low counter in his office, looking out at you through the small panes of the window. Later in the night, he would close the metal shutters inside the window, and you would see only the line of light in the crack between the shutters.

I was tired but content as my mother and I approached the Gate. The long walk along the Line had been a journey of companionship, my child's questions fading into a cocoon of silence warmed by my mother's presence.

And inwardly I was warmed by the remembered excitement of the day just done – Christmas Eve in the town, the shop windows glowing with lights and toys and small cribs, the sharp air ringing with greetings of 'Happy Christmas' and 'Many happy returns'. Most of all, I was warmed by the knowledge that Mammy had chosen me to share in the last-minute preparations for Christmas, that even now, as we trudged towards the gate, I was carrying the red cardboard box which was itself our 'Christmas box' – a gift to Mammy from Keane's shop, where she bought the messages every week. The red box held a Christmas cake, covered in hard white icing which bore the inscription 'Merry Christmas', just like they said in the comics. The Christmas box was free, and was doubly special for that reason. The man in the shop had tied the twine around the red box in such a way that it formed a loop to fit around my wrist, and did not cut my fingers at all. I had the small shopping-bag in my other hand. My mother was carrying three bags, each of them heavier than the one I carried.

I looked up at her as we stepped into the brightness of the big swan-necked light above the Gate. There were beads of sweat on her brow.

25

'I can take another bag, Mammy,' I said to her.

She shook her head. 'It's all right,' she said, 'sure we're nearly home now.'

We heard the big bolt being drawn back inside, and the great door of the Gate swung open before us.

'It's a hardy night, Mrs Brophy,' the PA said to my mother. The polished red peak of his military policeman's cap gleamed in the light. The brass buttons of his dark-green uniform shone like yellow gold.

'It is, to be sure, Jim,' my mother said, 'but sure it's dry anyway, thank God.'

'It is that,' Jim O'Dowd went on, 'it's good and dry for Santy to be on his rounds tonight.'

He smiled as he spoke, looking from my mother to me. I knew him for a kindly man – not at all like the other, larger PA, Bartley, who frequently and loudly threatened to put bold boys 'into the guard-room' – but not even his smile could quite remove the look of menace from Jim O'Dowd's face. It was no bluer, no flintier, nor more close-shaven than my father's; what lent that face its own particular fascination was the dimple in the chin. The dimple was wide and dark and bottomless. You could see into it but you were afraid to look too closely in case you fell into it or – more likely – gunfire erupted from it. Every boy in the barracks knew that Jim O'Dowd had taken a bullet smack in the middle of his chin. He had told us so himself, his hand resting on the flapped holster of his military policeman's pistol. The circumstances of the shoot-out were vague and therefore more mysterious. We knew instinctively that the bullet was still lodged there at the bottom of that wicked hole in his chin, that it would probably be fatal to have it removed.

'What's Santy bringin' you?' he asked me.

'A book,' I answered. I felt I had answered the same question at least a dozen times while shopping in the town with my mother. Grown-ups' conversation seemed to be decidedly limited, restricted as it was to such basic question-and-answer stuff.

'And what book is that?' he probed.

'I don't know,' I said, 'it's a surprise.'

I wondered if you could feel the bullet if you pushed one of my mother's knitting needles into the hole in his chin. Maybe if you pushed hard enough you could dislodge the bullet and force it out through the back of his neck.

'We'll have to be gettin' on, Jim,' my mother said. 'Mrs Folan is mindin' the rest of them.'

'Sure amn't I the terrible man keepin' you here like this,' the PA said, 'and you probably have a hundred things to do on Christmas Eve an' all.'

My mother's laugh tinkled in the small office. 'The only job left for doin' now,' she said, 'is to get them all to bed in time before Santy comes.'

'Oh, begod, but you're dead right, Mrs Brophy,' Jim said, his voice as mournful as his face. 'I was on duty many a Christmas Eve and d'you know what it is, but Santy always asks me if there's any house in the Barracks where the childer aren't in bed because he just won't come to any house like that, you know, he just won't come to it at all.'

'Will you be talking to Santy tonight?' I asked.

He nodded solemnly. 'He'll be standing there where you're standing yourself,' Jim intoned, 'warmin' his hands on that oul' stove there because he's often frozen stiff after the long journey with the reindeers from the North Pole.'

'The reindeers!' I breathed. 'Will you see them as well?'

'Of course I will. Sure amn't I on duty here at the Gate all night!'

Having a pistol and a red-peaked cap was not the only bonus that went with being a military policeman in the army.

'C'mon, Kevin,' Mammy said. 'The others'll be wonderin' where we are.'

There was a question I was bursting to ask. 'Was there ever a house in the Barracks,' I asked, 'that Santy didn't go to?'

Jim considered my question. The smile left his face and the hole in his chin seemed to grow wider and blacker. 'Only one,' he said. 'Only one house that I can remember Santy wouldn't go to.'

'Which house?' I whispered. 'Which house?'

'They don't live here anymore,' Jim said, 'they've gone out of the Barracks long ago.'

'But which house?' I persisted.

'Begod, now, I can't be sure . . .' Jim began.

'It wasn't Number 20, sure it wasn't, Jim,' my mother interrupted quickly.

'Ah sure, of course it wasn't Number 20,' Jim agreed hastily, 'sure how could it be Number 20? Doesn't everybody know that Number 20 is the first house in the Barracks that Santy goes to!'

I smiled at my mother in relief. She could always sense instinctively whatever threatened me and always knew how to disarm the darkness.

Jim opened the back door of his little office to admit us into the enclosed world of the Barracks. On our right loomed the grey fortress of the colonel's house, close at hand yet as remote and distant as the sanctuary of the church; beyond it the hoar frost was white on the lawn where the officers played tennis in the summer evenings, and across the lawn you could see the wide expanse of the Square, deserted now under the perimeter lights and the curtainless windows of the unmarried soldiers' billets.

The door of the Gate fell shut behind us. Mother and I walked in the shadow of the high barracks wall towards the two-storey building which comprised the Married Quarters. I looked up at the top of the armoury stores that we simply called the Magazine. The hard-edged outline of the empty flag-pole reached up towards the sky.

'We're late for the flag, Mammy,' I said. I felt my hand squeezed in hers.

'No matter,' she said. 'It's no harm to miss it for one day.' She knew how I loved the ceremony of the taking-down of the green, white and gold flag each evening.

'No,' I said, 'It's no harm.'

You couldn't have everything. If you lived in the Married Quarters you could play hurling with a sponge ball or a winder, but you had to be an officer to play tennis on the lawn.

There were steps leading down to the narrow forecourt that stretched in front of the entire length of the Married Quarters. It was unevenly surfaced with chipped and broken tarmac, an endless battleground of bloodied knees and scraped shins for the Barracks children who played there. On this Christmas Eve the stretch of ground was silent and empty. Through the windows of some of the ground-floor Quarters we could see mothers and children seated around the standard-issue army tables, having their tea and bread and butter. Some of the women waved through the window, and my mother called back a greeting to them.

My mother's pace quickened as we moved towards the Arch, the focal point of the Married Quarters. On this darkening Christmas Eve it was empty: the Dunne family, like most others, was indoors.

We climbed the stone staircase of the Arch to the upper level of the Married Quarters. From up here you could look clear across the roof of the soldiers' cookhouse to the army playing-fields and the dark waters of the bay, and the intermittent beacon of the lighthouse, flashing in the night.

We turned left towards Number 20. We were nearly home. The stillness of the Barracks cloaked me, pushed me towards my mother. I tugged at her coat. She stopped and looked down at me. I loved the way her black hair was turned up and back in a soft wave from her forehead. 'What is it?' she asked me.

Number 20 was only a few steps away, and I was anxious to be home and to be boasting to my sister and brother about the wonders of the day's shopping in town. Or was I? Some part of me wanted this shared day never to end, wanted this partnership of enchantment to continue forever, as if we could always stand there in the falling darkness on the veranda, the Barracks spread around us like an unroused giant, breathing quietly with its flag furled and its hands resting on its sated stomach.

'What is it?' she asked again.

'I don't know, Mammy,' I said.

She laughed and bent to kiss me. 'Don't worry,' she said. 'There'll be other days when we can go to town together.'

She could always read my mind.

My mother wasn't being strictly accurate when she told Jim O'Dowd that the only job left for doing on this Christmas Eve was to get the children to bed in time for Santa Claus. Before that, the Christmas candle had to be lighted.

We all knew that the candle was stored on top of the glass case in the kitchen, wrapped in a sheet of thick brown paper. Mammy had shown it to us two weeks earlier when she'd brought it from town, but we'd been forbidden to touch it. The three of us – my brother and sister and myself – watched intently as my mother stood on a chair and reached up over the glass case that housed our cups and saucers and plates to retrieve the candle. Her expression was solemn and unsmiling as she stepped down gingerly from the chair onto the linoleum. She held the wrapped-up candle out from her body like a sacred scroll.

'I hope it's not broken, Mammy,' my brother Jacky said.

My mother half-smiled at him. I said nothing. My three-year-old brother's conversation gambits were usually too daft to require further comment. In any case, I knew the candle wasn't broken: I'd sneaked a look the previous day when Mammy had gone across to the Folans' house for a chat.

'Don't worry, *a ghrá*,' my mother said, 'it's not broken.'

Sometimes I wondered why Mammy bothered to respond to such childish stuff, but on this occasion I kept my feelings to myself.

My mother laid the candle on the kitchen table and slowly unrolled it across the bare, scrubbed board. There was a silence as we watched the paper unwind across the table, until finally the candle was revealed, long and dark red and slender, sleeping on its sheet of thick waxed paper.

'Can I hold it, Mammy?' It was my sister, Miriam, who broke the silence in the kitchen. Her voice was uneven and breathy, a legacy of the pneumonia which had almost killed her in the autumn of that year. The bedroom we all shared had been kept dark while she'd been ill, with an old towel wrapped around the enamel light-shade.

My mother picked up the candle. 'Hold it carefully,' she said, placing it gently in Muriel's hands.

The red candle rested on the palms of her white hands. Under her blonde hair her face was pale. Her small chest rose and fell rapidly against the pink wool of her jumper. Her blue eyes never wavered from the candle resting across her hands. 'It's heavy,' she whispered. Miriam was only four, and she was a girl. 'It's heavy, Mammy.'

My mother took the candle from her. 'But it's lovely, isn't it?'

Miriam nodded. 'Yes, Mammy,' she breathed, 'it's lovely.'

Of course, Jacky had to be allowed to hold it after that, but I noticed that my mother kept her hands under his while the candle was in his possession. I even allowed Mother to place the candle briefly in my own hands, as I couldn't very well admit to having already conducted an unofficial inspection.

I was eager for the candle to be lighted and I said so.

'Try to be a bit more patient, Kevin. You don't have to go rushing at everything.' The rebuke was gentle, but tears stung at the corners of my eyes. 'The way you helped me with the messages,' she went on. 'Sure you were a great boy in the town, and you were very patient while I did the shopping.'

I smiled up at her. 'Will I get the baby, Mammy?' It was a way to make amends. It also demonstrated that I was really quite grown-up.

'Do,' she said. 'Just be careful lifting him up – like you always are.'

I hurried out of the kitchen into the stone-floored scullery. The scullery was long and narrow: at the far end was a brown delph sink where the dishes were washed and my father shaved and my mother washed our hair every Saturday night. Beside the sink was the door to the lavatory. The bedroom was off the scullery, at the back of the kitchen. There were two double beds in the room, one for us children, the other for my parents. The baby's pram was pushed up against the foot of my parents' bed. I peered into the pram in the dark room.

'He's asleep.' Miriam spoke at my elbow; she'd followed me from the kitchen.

It seemed to me to be a great pity not to leave him asleep – he was forever bawling for attention just when I was engaging Mother in conversation – but we'd been told repeatedly that even the baby had to be present for the lighting of the candle. I pushed the baby blankets down and bent over the pram. I sniffed carefully: there was nothing but the warm baby smell of sleep and powder. Slowly, as Mammy had demonstrated, I got my hands under the baby and lifted. I prayed hard that he wouldn't start crying, and Baby Jesus must have heard my prayers, for the baby cried only once when he opened his eyes and then promptly went back to sleep again in my arms.

I bore him like a trophy into the kitchen. Miriam padded behind me, carrying one of the baby blankets. 'You're a great boy,' Mammy said to me, taking the baby in her arms, 'and you're a great little girl,' she told Miriam, as she wrapped the sleeping baby in the blanket.

While we'd been in the bedroom, my mother had stood the candle in the specially cleaned jam-jar, packed round with tightly

31

wadded bits of newspaper. The jam-jar was covered in green crêpe-paper that hung in a cut fringe from the edge of the jar.

'Everybody ready?' Mammy asked.

We all answered yes eagerly. My mother stepped back and switched off the electric light. Now there was only the turf fire in the high grate to light the kitchen. Her face was softer than ever in the glow of the firelight, the baby clasped in her arms. Shadows flickered on the distempered walls of this room where we lived and talked and cooked and where we were now gathered around the white deal table. In the stillness that descended upon the kitchen you could hear Miriam's shallow breathing and the baby's purring noises of sleep. Was it the silence and the shadows that made my mother's voice seem different – or was it that she too could feel the sense of mystery that swept over me?

'You know why we're going to light the Christmas candle,' she said. 'Long ago in Bethlehem Joseph and Mary knocked on all the doors but nobody would let them in and give them a place to sleep. They had to take shelter in a stable and Baby Jesus was born there in the straw, along with the ass and the ox, and that was the very first Christmas night.' Mammy paused. I felt her shining eyes moving from me to Jacky to Miriam, standing around the table. 'We're going to light the candle and put it in the window so that Joseph and Mary will know that there's shelter for them and Baby Jesus in this house if they're travelling past our door tonight.' Mother held out the box of matches to Miriam. 'Everyone has to help lighting the candle,' she said. 'Pass the matches on to Kevin, Miriam.'

My sister took the small box from Mammy. She smiled shyly at me, then at Mammy. 'Can I take the match out, Mammy?' she asked. Mother nodded. Miriam pushed open the box, drew out one of the red-headed matches and handed me the match and the box.

'Shut the box first.' My mother's voice was quiet.

I did as she said and struck the match on the raspy side of the box. The sulphur head sizzled and flared. For an instant I held the match tilted downwards, as Mammy had shown me, until the flame steadied, and then I turned the matchstick upright.

'Now give it to Jacky – carefully.'

I followed her instructions reluctantly, but it was an unalterable part of our liturgy that the privilege of lighting the candle fell to the youngest in the house: in a couple of years the torch would have passed on to baby Danny.'

My three-year-old brother was standing on a chair. He took the lighted match with wide eyes and much indrawing of breath. Mammy's hand hovered at his elbow as he reached out to the candle. Her hand closed gently around his small wrist, guiding it toward the white wick.

The wick took flame. The candle was lighting.

Mammy took the dying match from Jacky's hand and blew it out.

'Now bless yourselves,' she said, crossing herself.

Miriam and I blessed ourselves with expansive gestures. My mother made the sign of the cross with her thumb on the baby's forehead. She bent towards Jacky and touched his face with her hand. 'You were very good lighting the candle,' she said softly, and he grinned up at her as she made the sign of the cross on his forehead.

I wasn't jealous. Growing up meant giving up some things. I recalled how Miriam had lighted the candle on another Christmas Eve, when we had lived in a barely remembered room in the town. The three of us waited while Mammy put the baby back into the pram in the bedroom. When she returned she lifted the lighted candle from the table and stepped across to the window. She set the jam-jar and candle down carefully on the deep, wooden window-sill. We watched her in silence.

'It's nice when the light is off.' It was my sister who spoke. I looked at her rapt face in surprise. I had been thinking the same thing.

'Are all the lights off in all the houses, Mammy?' I asked her.

'I don't know,' she said, 'but there'll be candles lighting in them all.'

I could see them in my mind – all the candles lighting in all the windows, so that Joseph and Mary would know there was plenty of room for them in the Married Quarters. It wasn't enough to see them merely in my mind. 'Can I go outside and see them, Mammy?'

'It's late and it's dark . . .'

'Please,' I begged her. 'Just for a minute.'

She relented. 'Just for a minute then – but put your coat on first.' She took my coat down from the black hook on the back of the kitchen door and handed it to me.

'Can I go too, Mammy?' Miriam's voice was small and piping.

Mother bent and picked my sister up in her arms. 'It's too cold for you, *a ghrá*,' Mammy said. 'Anyway, I want you to stay here and help me get the tea ready.' Her arms tightened around Miriam in an embrace that was fierce and loving. 'Will you help me?'

I heard Miriam say yes as I buttoned up my overcoat. 'I'm ready, Mammy,' I said.

'Now remember, it's only for a minute, and you're to hurry back.'

'I know, Mammy,' I said.

I hurried out of the kitchen. I opened our outside door and stepped into the hall that we shared with the family opposite. The hall was unlighted, but I could see well enough by the light of the Barracks lamps that came through the fanlight. The veranda was deserted. My pace quickened as I made my way down the stone staircase of the Arch. Opposite the Arch was a five-foot-high wall that separated the Married Quarters from the soldiers' area, but there was a familiar foothold in the wall that made the climbing easy, even in the dark.

After I crossed the wall I resolutely kept my back to the Quarters. I didn't want to see the lighted candles until I was ready. I hurried further away. I passed by the canteen, where the private soldiers went, and then by the corner of the NCOs' Mess. I counted out twenty steps from the mess until I stood in the open space of the parade ground. For a moment I stood silent in that vast desert of concrete. I took a deep breath and turned around.

The Married Quarters twinkled with the orange flames of Christmas candles in all the windows. Some, like Number 20, were in darkness, lighted only by the candles. Others had the curtains drawn, but the tiny pinpoints of light flickered like lighthouses in the windows. It seemed as if the whole barracks was holding its breath, waiting for Joseph and Mary to come passing by, looking for shelter for the night of Christmas Eve. Would Jim O'Dowd at the Gate tell them to go to Number 20, or would he more likely send them to his own house, in the upper level of the Arch? I wondered if Santy might meet them in the dark, and give them a lift along the way . . .

The golden lights swam before me in a blur. I shut my eyes, counted to three, and opened them again. The lights were steady once more. I tried to pick out the candle in Number 20 on the top deck of the veranda, but in the darkness I couldn't be sure. I thought again of Mary in her white dress and blue cloak and Joseph in his dark brown robe, and every door closed against them. Tonight our door would remain unlocked, the black iron key unturned.

Of a sudden I felt my own smallness, standing there on the silent parade ground, and I shivered in the darkness. I was glad my mother was up there in Number 20, getting the tea ready with Jacky and Miriam while the baby slept in his pram. I hurried home.

THREE

We moved to Number 2 in the Married Quarters. I missed the high-level living of Number 20, up on the veranda, but I quickly learned to appreciate the added status of our new home. We no longer shared the hallway, as in Number 20, with a family living opposite; the two rooms across the hallway, together with the extra scullery and lavatory, were ours.

I explained breathlessly to my pal, Paul O'Dowd – he was the son of Jim, in whose chin the bullet lay lodged – that living in Number 2 was just like having two houses to live in. We now had two lavs and two sculleries.

'And of course,' I said mysteriously to Paul, 'it *is* Number 2.'

I hadn't fully worked out either the mystery or the significance of this, but it had to mean *something*.

'And another thing,' I went on, 'my Dad has two stripes 'cos he's a sergeant.'

'That's a load of oul' codswallop,' Paul said, 'and has nothing to do with anything.' Paul was the same age as me. He had neither brothers nor sisters, but compensated by displaying the most adult vocabulary of our entire group.

'It isn't cods . . . codswallop', I said, enjoying the weight of the word, 'because we *do* have two lavs and my father *has* two stripes on his sleeve'.

Paul glared at me. 'Infantile codswallop,' he spluttered before striding off.

The O'Dowds lived at the top of the stairs in the Arch and had only one lav and one scullery. Furthermore, his shiny holster and bullet-hole chin notwithstanding, Paul's father had only one stripe on his sleeve because he was only a corporal. I decided against shooting this parting arrow after Paul's retreating back. It had, anyway, already been said between and behind my words – or else

36

why would Paul have gotten so angry? There was also the consideration that alienating him still more might jeopardise my loan of next week's *Eagle* from Paul. Silence, I reasoned, was the nobler attitude; it was no more Dan Dare's fault than Paul's own that he was stuck with a father who had only one stripe.

But I was puzzled by one thing. I hurried indoors to consult my mother. She knew the answer to everything.

I was already calling out the question to her as I pushed open the green door into the big kitchen of Number 2: 'Mammy, what's infantile codswallop?'

'Is that any way for a boy to come into his house, shouting at his mother?'

My mother was not alone. The question came from Granny Parsons. The sight of her, sitting in one of our wooden armchairs beside the shining range, drew me to a speechless stop inside the door.

'Well, is it? And I thought you were a mannerly little boy.'

Granny Parsons wore a long black shawl after the manner of the older women in the town; indoors, she let it slip down from her head so that it draped across her shoulders as for an occult benediction. I gazed in fascination at the hairs on her chin. My mother had hushed me, sternly, when I had once suggested that Granny Parsons should borrow my father's razor with the blue Gillette blade. I looked helplessly to my mother for support. Mammy was sitting in the other armchair, at the other side of the range. Between them sat Mrs Good, who lived upstairs on the veranda.

'What d'you want to know, *a ghrá*?' my Mother asked. There was a tiredness in her smile; her face was fuller now, and her tummy strained against the fabric of her apron.

'Infantile codswallop, Mammy,' I said, 'what is it?'

'The Lord save us,' Mrs Good intoned in her deep, mannish voice, 'but that child will come to a bad end. Infantile codswallop! I ask you!'

I felt myself engulfed by enlightenment. 'Is it a bad word, Mammy?'

My mother laughed, neatly tipping the ash from her Woodbine into the ashes box of the range. 'No, Kevin,' she said, 'it's not a bad word at all. Who said it to you?'

'Paul O'Dowd.'

'Oh, sure, who else would it be!' Mrs Good boomed again, her permed head shaking and her large bosom heaving. 'Another fellow who always has his head stuck in a book!'

'But what is it Mammy?' I persisted. 'What's infantile codswallop?'

'It just means nonsense – you know, like talking through your hat.'

'A bad end,' Mrs Good repeated, but I was heedless now.

'Codswallop is rubbish, Mammy.'

'That's right, *a ghrá*, that's what I'm telling you.'

'So what's infantile?' I asked in exasperation.

'I suppose it's just – you know – like an infant.' My mother seemed unsure of herself.

'Like a baby, sort of?'

'Yes, that's right, like baby-talk.'

''Cos they only talk rubbish, Mammy – babies, I mean.' I spoke from weary experience – how many times had Mammy broken off a perfectly intelligent conversation with me to indulge in ridiculous baby-talk with my brother, Danny?

'Babies have to learn how to talk,' Mammy said.

'I wish,' I said slowly, 'that Danny would learn quickly so that we don't have to put up with much more infantile codswallop from him.'

'It's not natural.' Granny Parsons stirred in her chair. She rearranged the folds of her shawl and drew it up around her head. 'It's not natural at all, talkin' about babies like that.'

'It's true for you, Mother,' Mrs Good agreed. Granny Parsons was Mrs Good's mother. (I had at first found it difficult to grasp that a grown-up could have – or need – a mother.) Even though Granny Parsons wore a shawl, she wasn't a tinker like the people in Tinker's Lane beside the chapel.

'Sure the lad meant no harm, Martha.' My mother used Granny Parsons' first name.

'It's still not natural,' Granny Parsons said from the folds of her shawl, 'for a young fellow to be talkin' to his mother about babies at this time.'

'At what time?' I cut in.

'Not natural at all, at all,' Mrs Good agreed, with a great sighing heave of her chest that covered my question with cushioning mountains.

'I was only asking about infantile codswallop,' I said, but I addressed my protestations to my mother's plump tummy rather than to Mrs Good's impressive bosom or to Granny Parsons' round, doughy face.

'Sure I know that,' my mother said to me. I felt her arms close around me and I levered myself up onto her lap.

'Will you for God's sake be careful, Mrs Brophy.' The voice from the shawl was sharp. 'You haven't that much time to go now.'

'Time to go where?' I asked, but only dreamily: my mother's lap was cosy and comfortable: when I looked up at her I felt the warmth of her eyes and I snuggled closer. 'Time to go where?' I repeated.

'Time for you to leave your poor mother in peace,' Mrs Good said. 'C'mon now, off with you.'

My mother started to protest, but Mrs Good stood up and, gently but firmly, lifted me from my mother's lap.

'He's only – '

'He's only going outside to play for a while!' Mrs Good cut off my mother. Mrs Good's hand rested on my shoulder. I felt the heat at my back as I stood in the confined arc between the chairs and the range.

'I don't particularly want to go out to play,' I said. The October evening was chilly; the breeze had an edge to it, blowing down from the barracks gate. Granny Parsons snorted: the black shawl shook with indignation.

'You can play in the room with your brother and sister,' my mother said. The 'room' was the unused back bedroom on the other side of our hallway. 'But leave the baby asleep,' Mammy added. My baby brother still slept for part of every afternoon; my parents' bedroom – the front room across the hall – was therefore out of bounds.

I weighed up the choice between the chilly darkening evening and the combination of girlish chatter from Miriam mixed with infantile codswallop from my brother Jacky. 'Okay,' I told them, 'I'll go out to play.'

I wasn't quick enough in recoiling from Mrs Good's descending bosoms. They squashed against my nose as her arms went round me. I was surprised to find that, after the initial shock to my senses, the bosoms not only felt comfortable, but they also smelt of an inviting softness. I felt a slight, unexpected pang of regret when she pushed me from her. 'I knew you were a good boy after all,' she said to me.

'Of course he's a good boy,' my mother chimed in.

The black shawl merely snorted.

'Your Mammy is just a bit tired and she just needs to sit and chat for a while,' Mrs Good added.

I nodded. I was tired of this conversation which went round in diminishing circles.

'So long, Mammy,' I said, like Kit Carson in the 64-page comics.

'Say goodbye to Mrs Good and Granny Parsons,' my mother told me.

'So long, Mrs Good, so long, Granny Parsons.'

They'd be scalped in no time at all, I figured, if they ever strayed off from Kit's wagon-train, although Granny Parsons, in her black shawl, might be able to disguise herself as a squaw until Kit came riding to the rescue. Anyway, she wasn't my Granny, and I couldn't make up my mind as to whether I should tell her how to survive a Sioux attack.

'Close the door easy so you don't waken the baby, Kevin.'

I nodded to my mother, gave her a casual wave of my left hand, like Kit hitting the trail, and stepped out of the warm kitchen into the stone-floored scullery.

A week later I came running up the hallway of Number 2, unbuckling my school-bag from my shoulders as I ran. 'Mammy, I'm home – '

'Whisht! Whisht! Let you be quiet!' Mrs Good turned from the sink in the scullery where she was filling the kettle. Her eyes glared at me from behind her tortoise-shell glasses.

'Where's Mammy?' I asked, puzzled by Mrs Good's presence.

'She's not feeling well, she's in bed.'

'But I have to get my dinner after coming home from school.' Anticipation of a chat with Mammy while I ate my dinner always hurried me home along the Line.

'You'll *get* your dinner,' Mrs Good said, passing me in the scullery. 'I'll get it for you myself.' She levered the circular lid from the top of the range and set the big, swan-necked kettle down on top of the flames.

'I want to see Mammy!' I dropped my school-bag on the floor and turned impulsively towards the kitchen door. Mrs Good's speed across the floor astonished me. She pushed the door closed and turned to face me.

'You can't see her. She's in bed 'cos she's not feeling well.'

'I want to see my Mammy!' I tried to grab the brass door-knob, but Mrs Good caught me by the wrist.

'You can't see her,' she said firmly, 'and that's that! Now sit down and I'll get you your dinner!'

At that moment the door opened behind her. Granny Parsons stood there with her sleeves rolled up. I had never before seen her without her shawl. She wore a patterned, grey wrap-around smock that seemed to emphasise her roundness. 'I hope you're not going to be a troublesome boy.'

Her piping voice cowed me. 'What's wrong with Mammy?'

'She's just not well,' Granny Parsons said. 'She has to stay in bed for a while.'

'When will she be better?' I asked. 'Will she be up at tea-time?'

'She'll be up when she's better, *a mac*,' Granny Parsons said, 'so sit up there now like a good ladeen and you'll get your dinner.'

I allowed myself to be propelled gently towards the table by Mrs Good. I sat and watched while she cut a slice off the brown cake and another off the currant-cake that my mother had baked the previous day. 'We get spuds for our dinner,' I said to her. 'The cake is for tea-time.'

'You're getting cake for your dinner today,' Mrs Good said, 'or else you can go hungry.' She buttered the two slices of cake and set them on the yellow-squared oil-cloth in front of me. I watched while she poured the mug of tea and added milk and two spoonfuls of sugar. She stirred the sugar into the tea and placed the mug beside the two cuts of cake.

'Aren't you hungry after school all day?'

I stared at the oil-cloth that covered the table. My mother had bought it when we'd moved downstairs to Number 2. 'I wish Mammy was here.' I'd watched her tuck the oil-cloth neatly under the edge of the table and pin it all around with thumb-tacks.

'It's only for a while that you can't see her, Kevin. It won't be long.'

'She *will* get better? She's not going to die like John Cotter?' John Cotter lived in the Quarters upstairs, almost right over Number 2, and he'd died the day before.

Mrs Good's face eased itself into a half-smile. 'No,' she said, 'your Mammy is not going to die.'

'Honest?'

'Honest.'

'Cross your heart and hope to die?'

Mrs Good's right index-finger traced a cross over her left bosom. 'She won't,' she said. 'Granny Parsons has never lost one yet.'

I was mystified. 'Was Mammy lost?'

'I only meant that Granny Parsons is the best in the world at looking after Mammies when they're not well.'

I moved one of the slices of cake so that it sat plumb centre on top of the red rose in a square of the table-cloth. 'Does she look after loads of Mammies?'

'Loads of them.'

'And she never – ' I settled my tongue around the intriguing expression – 'lost one of them?'

'Never,' Mrs Good replied in a tone of reverence, like the priest saying Amen.

'Did she ever have to go looking for one of them?'

I'd never seen Mrs Good laugh before. Her strapped-up bosoms heaved against her pink cardigan as she shook with laughter. Adults were truly beyond comprehension; you asked a perfectly reasonable question and Mrs Good behaved as if you'd told a funny story.

'No, *a mac*,' she said, 'she never had to go looking for a Mammy that needs her. There's always plenty of Mammies in trouble, though, that come looking for her.' She started to shake once more with laughter, although I couldn't see what was so funny. I watched her fold her arms across her chest and visibly subdue her quivering bosoms into stillness. 'You're a terror for the questions,' she said to me. 'You better watch yourself that all them questions don't land you in trouble some day.'

I took a bite from the slice of currant-cake. When I left it down on the table-cloth you could see the red rose showing through the space where I'd bitten. 'What kind of trouble?'

'Musha, lay me alone, yourself and your questions.' Mrs Good moved towards the door. 'I'm going in to see your mother.'

'Why can you see her and I can't?'

'That's the why,' Mrs Good said.

'Where are the others?' I called after her. 'Where're Miriam and Jacky?'

'They're out next door in the Folans' and the baby – '

– is asleep,' I finished for her. The baby was always asleep, except when he was being fed or having his nappy changed. Babies were pretty useless: you had to keep quiet when they were asleep but whenever *they* were awake they could shout their heads off.

'He's a *good* baby,' Mrs Good said with emphasis. The door closed behind her. I heard the door into the hall being opened and closed and then, more faintly, the sound of the *other* hall door opening and closing as Mrs Good stepped into the second scullery that led into the bedroom where they wouldn't let me see my mother. Two families could live here. I'd heard my mother describe Number 2 as a 'double quarters'.

The kitchen seemed empty. It had been its usual busy self that morning when I'd had my bowl of porridge and put my sandwiches, wrapped in grease-proof paper, into my school-bag. Now the blue clock on the mantelpiece ticked loudly in the emptiness and even the children's programmes on the wireless didn't start until five o'clock. That was an hour away. I finished my slices of cake and drank my tea slowly. Time ticked by with maddening slowness in the kitchen. When I looked again at the clock the long hand still hadn't reached five past the hour. I had lessons to learn, but they were only Irish and English spellings, and I knew them already. I decided to call for Art Folan, who lived in Number 1, next door to us. My mother had said to my father that morning that John Cotter was laid out upstairs in his own bed. Art and myself would go and see him.

You had to go around the gable end of the Quarters to get to Art Folan's house. The door of Number 1 was hidden away around the corner of the block, with its own private view of the barracks coalyard. The gates of the yard, high as the barracks perimeter wall, were closed and padlocked.

Two steps led up to the door of Number 1. The house seemed unfinished to me, lacking the approach of our long hall at Number 2. Here at Art's house, when the front door was opened, you were, disconcertingly, immediately looking into the Folans' kitchen, just off a small porch where coats were hung.

Art himself opened the door. He had brownish hair and his face was covered with freckles. I envied him those freckles. Umpteen inspections in my father's shaving mirror had failed to produce a single freckle on my own disappointing face.

'Are you coming up to see John Cotter?' I asked him.

'He's dead,' Art said.

'I know,' I said. 'He's laid out.'

'What's "laid out"?'

I shrugged. 'Dunno. I heard my mother saying it.'

'You think we should investigate?'

I nodded. When we played cowboys around the barracks, Art and I often investigated murder scenes where some no-good bushwhackers had plugged some unarmed nester full of lead and left his body for the buzzards.

Just then Art's mother appeared behind him. Taller than Art's father, she was a private woman who kept herself to herself. 'Where are ye off to?' Mrs Folan asked.

Art's surreptitious finger on his lips signalled discretion. 'Just out for a while, Mammy,' he said.

Mrs Folan turned her attention to me. 'How's your Mammy?' she asked.

'She's sick. She's in bed.'

'I know. Your brother and sister are here.' Behind Mrs Folan I could see Miriam and Art's sister, Mary, playing with a couple of dolls. 'Did she get the doctor?'

'No, only Mrs Good and Granny Parsons are there.'

'Ah, she'll be all right so, if Mrs Parsons is there,' Mrs Folan said.

'I know,' I said. 'She never lost one yet.'

'What?' Art's mother's tone was sharp. 'What did you say?'

'Mrs Good told me,' I said solemnly. 'She never lost one yet.'

Mrs Folan shook her head, laughing. She had a pleasant face and white hair. 'Come back with P.J. for your tea,' she said. She still called Art by his old name, but everybody called him Art because he was Art in a play at school. 'I'm only after putting two appletarts in the oven this minute.' Mrs Folan's tarts were nearly as good as Mammy's, but she put caraway seeds into them and sometimes the seeds got stuck between your teeth.

She reached out to do up the buttons on Art's jumper. Your mother always put one or two buttons on the left shoulder when she was knitting you a jumper. 'Off with ye so,' she said.

Art's eyes rolled heavenward when he had closed the door. 'Squaws,' he said.

'Heap big trouble,' I said.

'Let's saddle up and hit the trail,' Art said. We grabbed the reins of our trusty horses and swung our right legs up and over the saddle. 'Easy, pardner,' Art said to his horse, patting him on the neck. A horse was a cowboy's best friend and you had to treat him right. 'Ready?'

'I'm ready, Art.'

'Let's move out.'

When you were riding around the western plains of the Barracks, you had to lean your head forward so that you could whisper encouragement into your horse's ear. You held your left arm parallel to the ground, bent at the elbow, with the reins gripped loosely in front of your chest, in your left hand. When you wanted your horse to go faster – especially if a war-party of Injuns was in hot pursuit – you slapped yourself on the bottom with your right hand.

We cantered easily around the corner and on past Number 2. The curtains were drawn on the two high windows of my parents' bedroom. As I rode past, chatting to Art, part of my mind could see my mother lying in the big bed while Granny Parsons hovered alongside, like a black-shawled medicine-man, chanting incoherent spells. We reined in at the Arch, to give our mounts a breather before tackling the hills.

Mrs Dunne was standing at the foot of the stairs in the Arch, arms folded across her smock. It was hard to get up or down the stairs without Mrs Dunne seeing you. 'Where are ye two off to?' Sometimes I thought that Mrs Dunne stood there even throughout the night, keeping watch on movements through the Arch.

'We're going up to see – '

'We're on a mission,' Art interrupted me. 'We have to go and investigate something.'

Mrs Dunne's features betrayed no emotion. 'What kind of a mission?'

'It's top secret,' Art said. 'Forward-ho!' he waved our cavalry column forward up the stairs.

'How's your mother?' I heard her voice calling up after me as our horses negotiated the steep ascent.

'She's in bed,' I called back, without turning round, careful to help my mount pick his way along a particularly tricky slope. 'Granny Parsons is with her.'

Whatever Mrs Dunne shouted after that I couldn't hear, for by then our tired horses had crested the final hill and we stood panting on the veranda. Beyond, in the falling darkness, lay the Black Hills of Dakota and the plains of Wyoming.

Art and I swung right along the veranda, away from Number 20, where I used to live. 'Let's go on foot from here,' I said to Art. 'The camp might be guarded.'

We dismounted and tethered our horses to the green veranda railings. Our boots would have clumped noisily on the smooth surface of the veranda had we not tied canvas sandbags around our feet to deaden the sound of our approach. We ducked under the lighted windows of the Suttons' and the Stantons'. You had to be careful in case them pesky Injuns had posted look-outs around their camp. Hugging the stone wall for cover we got past the Goods' without being observed.

At the last hallway on the veranda we straightened up and looked at each other. This L-shaped hallway housed the entrances to three separate quarters. The Cotters' door was positioned on the angle of the L, so at least we didn't have to venture into the airless gloom that surrounded the entrances to the two quarters at the furthest end of the hallway.

'Who'll go in first?' Art asked me.

'We'll go together,' I said, my voice quavering like Art's.

Reluctantly, we pushed open the door that led from the veranda into the hallway. It was brighter than we expected: the Cotters' door hung open and the light from their scullery spilled out into the hallway. Maybe you had to leave the door open when somebody was laid out.

We dithered at the open door. Alone among the families of the barracks, the Cotters had no children, and neither Art nor I had ever been inside their house. We could hear, indistinctly, the voices of adults coming from the kitchen. Since the layout of all the quarters was the same, I knew that the door across the scullery, slightly ajar, led into the bedroom.

That door slowly opened inwards and a huge figure filled the doorway, momentarily blocking the light. It was Seamus Costello. Seamus lived in one of the Quarters at the deepest end of the hallway. He was a cook in the Officers' Mess. The stained white apron which he often wore over his army trousers on his journeys between the Quarters and the Mess was missing: his green tunic, stretched across his massive chest, was buttoned up to the neck.

'Do ye want to see him?' Seamus's words were slowly and precisely enunciated, as if he were learning how to speak.

I nodded, and asked in a whisper: 'Is he laid out?'

Seamus's huge head moved slowly up and down. 'He is indeed,' he said, 'he is laid out in his own bed'. The way Seamus spoke it sounded like 'He iss laid out in hiss own bed', but on this occasion it didn't strike me as amusing. 'C'mon, boys.' He took us by the hand and led us into the bedroom. 'There he iss'.

John Cotter lay in his bed with his fair hair combed and neatly parted on one side. I had never seen two sheets on a bed, and I noticed how the top sheet was folded back so that the dead man's hands rested on it. A pair of rosary beads had been entwined in those still hands. A small crucifix rested on his chest.

My gaze moved slowly up to his face. John Cotter's vacant eyelids stared back at me. 'Why are his eyes closed?' I whispered.

'Sure why would he have them open now?' I heard Seamus say, but I kept my eyes fixed on the grey-white eyelids. 'Let ye kneel down,' Seamus said, 'and say a Hail Mary for him.'

Art and I knelt together beside the bed, although we took care not to touch it. We whispered the prayer, more or less in unison, and looked up at Seamus.

'That'll do,' he said. 'Let ye go home now.'

We rose with alacrity. The little man in the bed was as neatly arranged and folded as any of my sister's dolls, but he was more menacing than the hairless corpse of any settler left to rot in the desert by the Apaches. He was a small, quiet man who passed by Number 2 a few times a day, his green army cap perched like an opened envelope on top of his carefully slicked hair. He and I had never spoken to each other and I no longer wished to be with him in this sickly-sweet room.

Seamus led us out. Behind the closed door of the kitchen the drowsy voices droned on. I realised then that they were murmuring in prayer.

Outside, on the veranda, Seamus settled a large hand on my shoulder. He drew Art towards him with the other hand. 'None of the other childer came,' he said. 'What did ye come for?'

I looked across the roofs of the Stores that stood opposite the Married Quarters. It was still half-bright, but the moon was hanging in the sky, pale and barely visible, like some kind of assistant sun. 'I never saw anybody laid out,' I said.

'He's up in heaven now,' Seamus said ponderously. 'The angels came for him in his sleep.'

Heaven was up there beyond the two pale orbs in the sky, but you couldn't see it until you were dead and your eyes were closed forever and ever. I shivered and folded my arms across my jumper.

Seamus took some change from his pocket and held out two pennies towards us. 'One each,' he said. 'Buy a penny bar.'

I stole a furtive glance up at the big man. He never said much either to the kids or to the adults, when he passed by, going to or from work. If he passed close to you, you could often hear him humming or singing to himself.

'Take the pennies,' he said, 'and let ye not tell anybody who gave ye them.'

Seamus's nickname was 'Capall', but none of the boys ever said it to his face. A *capall* was a horse in Irish. Seamus was the most powerful swimmer in the Barracks: he could swim all the way out to the lighthouse and back again without stopping to get his breath.

'Off home with ye now.'

We left him then, clutching our pennies. We went in silence, neither saddling up our horses nor taking evasive action around the Injun encampments along the way. The Oregon trail had disappeared and we walked in the grey shadows of the Barracks buildings. The Arch was empty and cheerless without Mrs Dunne's sentinel presence.

I stopped outside Number 2.

'My mother said you have to come to our house to get your tea.' Art's words were the first spoken since we had left Seamus.

'I know,' I said, 'but I want to go in home first.'

'Will I come in with you?'

I shook my head. 'I'll be around in a minute.'

I watched Art go around the corner to his own house before I pushed open the door of Number 2. I wanted to see my mother.

This time I knew better than to head for the kitchen. At the end of the hall I opened the door to the right, leading into our spare scullery. Even as the brass knob rattled in my hasty hands I could hear the noises of chase gathering force in the kitchen, as Mrs Good hurried to head me off. She was too slow.

I had to blink against the light in my mother's room. Granny Parsons' mouth hung open, startled by my intrusion. She was standing on the far side of the bed, beside the wash-stand with the big white basin set in the hole of the stand, and the tall white jug beside it. I heard Mrs Good's panting behind me and felt her restraining hand on my shoulder. 'I couldn't stop him – '

Granny Parsons cut her off. 'Sure it's no harm now,' she said quietly. 'Let the lad see his mother.'

My mother's head rested on two pillows angled against the grey iron headrail of the army bedstead. Her uncombed hair was matted like black foliage on the white pillows. Pearls of perspiration glistened on her forehead. She opened her eyes and I knew she wasn't dead.

'Kevin.' Her voice came from a far distance. She lifted her hand a little from the grey blanket that covered her and gestured me towards her.

I hung back, my fingers tightening on the brass door-knob.

'Go over and kiss your mother.' I hardly heard Granny Parsons' words. Mrs Good propelled me towards the bed and my mother smiled, a tired smile, and John Cotter's ashen face faded from my mind.

My mother's hand closed around mine. 'Are you better now, Mammy?' I whispered.

She nodded: the mass of black hair stirred on the pillow. 'I'm grand now, *a ghrá*.'

'Your face is sweaty,' I said.

'I'm a bit tired, that's all.' Her fingers slackened on my hand. I wondered why Granny Parsons and Mrs Good didn't go away and leave my mother alone.

'Will you be getting up for tea, Mammy?'

My mother laughed. 'Aren't you going to look at your new baby sister?'

As if on cue, the sound of a baby's crying came from beside her. I hadn't seen the baby, wrapped in a pink blanket, lying on the other side of my mother. Mrs Good prised my fingers from my mother's hand and led me around the bed until I stood beside the small pink bundle. It didn't stop crying.

'What d'you think?' my mother asked.

I was thinking that we already had a baby. I was thinking that the house would never be quiet again, that now it would be practically impossible ever again to have a proper conversation with my mother.

I said: 'Why did you get a new baby?' I heard Granny Parsons tut-tutting behind me and knew I had said the wrong thing. I didn't care. 'Why?' I asked again.

My mother looked from me to the pink bundle. The baby had a wizened red face and black hair that pushed out under its pink shawl. It looked like Granny Parsons. 'Because the angels brought her to me,' my mother said.

'Leave your mother alone now,' Granny Parsons said, taking me by the arm.

'I want to stay with my Mammy,' I said petulantly, trying to shake her off.

Her fingers bit into my arm with surprising ferocity. 'Out!' she said. 'Your mother is tired.'

You couldn't resist adults. They pushed you around and there was nothing you could do about it. At the door of the bedroom I swung round to look again at my mother. Her eyes were closed and her face was tired as if she had travelled a long journey.

'Mammy?' I called her name softly and her eyes opened.

'What is it, *a ghrá*?'

'What's the baby's name, Mammy?'

Her pale blue eyes moved upwards from me to Granny Parsons. I had to strain to hear her softly-spoken reply. 'The baby's name is Martha,' she said.

Granny Parsons drew in her breath with an urgent sucking noise. 'Thank you,' she said in a harsh whisper. She released my arm and I watched her bend over the bed and raise my mother's hand to her lips. She kissed the hand greedily before laying it again on the blanket. 'Thank you,' she said again. There were tears in her eyes when she straightened, and I turned away from her.

'So long, Mammy,' I said.

She didn't answer. She was asleep again.

The Barracks lights were on when I stepped outside. Mrs Folan had apple-tart waiting around the corner but I lingered a while on our doorstep, my mind wandering in circles. There were millions of stars in the sky at night, and the sky always looked the same, but you couldn't be sure it was the same. You could never count all the stars in the sky, and anyway you couldn't tell if they were always in the same spot. Stars were like angels, they went on forever, doing God's bidding. The angels came down from heaven to collect John Cotter's soul and they came down to bring my mother a new baby, but you couldn't tell if it was the same angels who did both jobs. Maybe God had one lot of angels for collecting souls and another bunch for delivering babies. Maybe the crowd of angels bringing John Cotter's soul up to Heaven passed the other bunch on their way down with the new baby. They could have stopped for a chat, the two crowds of angels, under the light of a star, before going on their different ways, one lot back to Heaven and the other crowd to the Barracks. You couldn't explain some things, like calling a new baby after an old woman that wore a shawl . . .

I dawdled my way around the corner to the Folans', my hands in my trouser pockets. Naturally I'd have to tell Art and Miriam and the rest of them that I had a new baby sister, but I wouldn't tell them she was going to be named after Granny Parsons. Some information was best kept to yourself, for a while anyway. Besides, it was in the baby's best interests.

FOUR

'Leave my books alone!'

Seconds earlier my brother Jacky had been seated opposite me, spooning up his porridge at the kitchen table; now, with his innate gift for troublesome bi-location, he was suddenly seated on the lino-covered floor beside my chair, my school-bag open on his lap and my English book dangling from his porridgy fingers.

Pushing back my chair, I angrily grabbed the book and school-bag from him. Jacky struggled noisily, but I was too strong for him. 'You're after putting porridge stains on the cover of my English book!' I shouted at him. I felt the tears of frustration stinging my eyes. Fat globules of porridge were congealing on the ivory-coloured marbled wallpaper that Mammy had so lovingly cut and fitted as a cover on my English book. 'You're always doing stupid things anyway!' I cried at him.

Jacky climbed to his feet beside my chair. His thick black hair was cut tight around his impish face. I could never see why everybody chuckled at his stupid antics. 'I'll clean it,' he said, attempting to wrest the book from me.

'Go away!' I shouted. 'Just go away!' I pushed him and he fell backwards, landing on his bottom. I glanced guiltily over at my mother, who was brushing Miriam's hair beside the range.

Mammy paused in mid-stroke, the brush poised above Miriam's long golden hair. Our eyes met and I blushed. 'Don't be so rough to your small brother, Kevin,' she said sharply.

'It's not fair,' I protested. 'He's after putting porridge – '

'Just don't be so rough with him,' Mammy cut in. 'He's only four.'

Sensing sympathy, Jacky began to cry. 'Kevin knocked me down!' he wailed. 'Kevin knocked me down!'

I could have throttled him, seated on the shiny linoleum with his mouth back to his ears, screeching in such a voice that he could be heard outside the barracks gate.

'This place is like a flamin' zoo!' My father's voice filled the kitchen. He stood in the scullery doorway, glaring at us. Half of his face was still creamed with soapy lather. He held his silver razor in his right hand. 'Can't I even have peace here while I'm shavin' myself?'

My mother looked at him, but said nothing. The only sounds in the kitchen were the swishing noises of the brush on Miriam's hair and my father's angry breathing. You could see his powerful chest heaving against his white vest.

'Well?' My father still stood in the doorway, demanding an answer from the silent kitchen.

'They're only childer,' my mother said simply. She went on brushing my sister's hair. Sometimes Miriam cried when Mammy brushed out the tangles in her long, fine hair but now she was silent, her eyes downcast.

My father snorted. We felt his eyes upon us, moving from Mammy and Miriam beside the range, across the floor-bound figure of Jacky, quiet now, sucking a finger, on to the kitchen table where my baby brother, Danny, and myself were still seated. The blue-striped milk jug stood out like a beacon on the table amid a sea of bread-crumbs and the emptied vessels of tea-mugs and porridge-bowls.

'I just hope this place is going to look a bit different for the inspection today,' my father said grimly. With that he closed the door and went back to finish shaving himself at the sink in the scullery.

My eyes lingered on the closed door and the brass knob shining like a ball of gold. It gleamed so that you could see yourself, grotesque and distorted, in its curved surface.

I forced my glance towards my mother. She continued with her brushing, her left hand holding Miriam's head steady, her right hand moving the brush with firm strokes through the long, straight hair. She sat on the edge of the kitchen chair, her own back as straight as the rails on the chair's curved back. You could see the concentration in the firm set of her wide mouth and the clarity of her blue eyes, but you could see no sign of any resentment of my father's words.

'Mammy?' It was Miriam who broke the silence in the kitchen.

'I won't hurt with the tangles,' Mammy said, 'and anyway, amn't I nearly finished now?'

'It's not that,' Miriam said. A half-formed word stumbled from her mouth, and then she stopped, as if unsure how to continue.

My mother ceased her brushing. She took Miriam's pale face in her two hands and tilted her head upwards. 'What is it?' she asked.

'It's the house, Mammy,' Miriam said. She paused to draw breath and then the words tumbled from her. 'The house is lovely, Mammy, for the inspection, I mean – it's really lovely.'

It was uncanny how my soppy five-year-old sister instinctively came out with the words of wisdom and reassurance that I, from my vantage-point of nearly seven years, so often felt in my heart but was so rarely able to utter. I watched the anxious way in which she looked up into Mammy's face and had to admit that, for all the time she spent playing with her stupid dolls, Miriam might, nevertheless, be worth her place on one of the long wagon-trains that Kit Carson led through the Injun-infested lands of the Wild West.

'Sure don't I know it's lovely,' Mammy said quietly. 'Weren't you a great help to me with all the cleanin' and the shinin' and the polishin'?'

Miriam smiled shyly. 'I betcha the officers will say it's the nicest house in the inspection, Mammy,' she said.

'Yes!' I cut in. 'I bet it's the best house in the whole Married Quarters!'

'Ah now, I don't know about that,' Mammy said. 'Sure everybody'll have their house shinin' like a new pin today.' But you could see the pleasure lighting up her face at the thought of her pre-eminence. And anyway I *knew* that my mother was the best in the Married Quarters at everything from making rhubarb tarts to knitting jumpers. It simply stood to reason that Number 2 would be the best in the inspection.

'It's nicer than anybody else's house in the Quarters, Mammy,' I said to her.

She smiled across at me, but said nothing. She tucked Miriam's hair behind her ears with a few hair-grips and then tied the primrose-coloured ribbon around it, arranging the ribbon in a wide bow on the top of her head.

'There now,' Mammy said with satisfaction. 'That's you ready for school.' Only Miriam and myself were as yet going to school.

'What's the 'spection?' Jacky asked from his position on the floor.

'It's the *in*spection,' I volunteered. I sometimes doubted if my nuisance of a kid brother would ever be fit for school. 'It's when the officers come around to inspect the Married Quarters.'

'Are they goin' to insect our house, Mammy?' Jacky asked.

'*Inspect*,' I said, 'not *insect*. An insect is something you can step on.'

'It can be *insect* too,' Jacky objected. 'Can't it be *insect*, Mammy?'

'No, it can't!' I exploded. 'The word is – '

'That's enough of that now.' The firmness in my mother's voice silenced me. 'Give me that book, Kevin,' she went on, 'till I clean it.'

I handed her the porridge-stained English book. 'There,' I said, pointing at the cover, 'and there. The Brother will give out about the stains.'

My mother lifted the bottom of her apron and began to rub the cloth gently on the wallpaper of the book. Most of the marks disappeared under the first few rubs. She lifted the book close to her face and spat a small amount of spittle onto the cover. Then she began again her gentle rubbing with the apron-end on the damp cover. Within moments she held the book out to me. 'Now,' she said, 'it's like new again.'

And it was. She could make all things new with a rub of a cloth, just as she had made Number 2 shine like a palace for the inspection that would take place later in the day.

'Thanks, Mammy,' I said.

'And you,' she said, turning to Jacky, 'are not to go at your brother's school-bag again. Just leave those books alone.'

Out of sight, behind her back, I stuck my tongue out at Jacky.

'Kevin stuck his tongue out, Mammy! Kevin stuck his tongue out!' he screeched.

'Tell-tale-tattler!' I snarled at him, but I moved smartly away and out of reach of a possible clip on the ear from Mammy. I put the book back into my school-bag and buckled the bag shut.

'God give me patience with the lot of ye.' My mother spoke in a near-whisper. I looked across at her and saw the exasperation in her eyes. Her shoulders sagged; the ramrod straightness had left her spine.

'Sorry, Mammy,' I said.

'It's all right, *a ghrá*,' she said, shaking her head sadly. 'I just don't know why ye always have to be disagreeing with one another.'

I was contrite. 'Sorry, Mammy,' I repeated lamely.

She visibly shook herself, and straightened herself in the chair. 'Have ye both got yeer sandwiches?' Miriam and I nodded to her. 'And ye have the bus-fares?' We each held up our penny for the bus-ride into town. There was a new bus service between the town and the Barracks.

'Off with ye so. Bless yeerselves on the way out.'

The blue alarm-clock on the mantelpiece said twenty minutes to nine. The bus would not leave from outside the Barracks gate for another ten minutes but Mammy chivvied us into gathering up our school-bags and making haste.

'Kathleen Cullen missed the bus yesterday, Mammy,' Miriam said. Kathleen lived in a farmer's cottage further out the Line. We'd watched as Kathleen ran, red-faced and panting, after the slowly moving bus but Hysey, the beetle-browed conductor, was deaf to our shouted entreaties and the bus had pulled away, leaving the girl to walk the Line into town.

'Well, let ye not miss it now,' Mammy said. Her hand rested lightly on Miriam's shoulder and then I felt the familiar but fleeting touch of her fingers on my hair. These were her gestures of farewell.

'Will the inspection be over when we get home, Mammy?' I asked her.

'I don't know,' she said. 'It depends on what time they start and which end of the Quarters they begin at.'

'But they should begin at the Folans,' I said, 'because they're Number 1.'

My mother smiled. 'That'd be too sensible,' she said. 'Now for God's sake, will ye go,' she went on, 'it's nearly a quarter to.' Her smile gave the lie to her clucking disapproval, but Miriam and I moved towards the door. My sister dipped her finger in the holy-water font that hung beside the light-switch and blessed herself with pious determination, her eyes closed and her lips moving as she mouthed the words of the Sign of the Cross.

I blessed myself with the holy water, but more rapidly than my sister: men had to be tougher and more nonchalant about such activities. For a last time I let my glance roam over the shining kitchen, almost as if I had never seen it before, as if I might never see it again. Every surface gleamed from my mother's polishing. The two tall windows shone in the spring sunlight like mirrors. The curtains hung in crisp folds, freshly laundered, tied at the waist with ribbons of purple. My father's hurling and football medals were pinned like jewels on a shield-shaped piece of plywood that Mammy had covered with a length of soft black velvet – the shield rested on top of the dark chest of drawers that stood against the near wall of the kitchen. On the wall above the shield hung a picture of the county hurling team (my father was kneeling on one knee at the extreme right of the portrait) and not far from it was the picture of the Sacred Heart, with the little red lamp lighting in front of it. Truly, I thought, my home was a palace, and the gleaming black-and-silver range was like a throne.

'Kevin!' My mother's voice cut in on my thoughts. 'Will you stop your day-dreamin' and be off to school!'

I saw the laughter in my mother's eyes and felt Miriam's fingers slip into mine. 'C'mon,' she said, her pale blue eyes wide and serious. She opened the door into the scullery and we called our goodbyes back over our shoulders. Mammy and Jacky and Danny shouted final goodbyes after us: my father was standing at the sink at the far end of the scullery, drying his face with the white army towel. We called out goodbye to him as we turned into the hallway, and I thought the towel stirred in a token of valediction.

On the bus everybody was talking about the inspection.

'The general is coming from Dublin,' Bobby Dunne said, 'I heard Mammy telling my father.' This was news. If Mrs Dunne said it, then it came from solid sources.

Paul O'Dowd shook his head in disagreement. 'Dad reckoned it'll just be the brass from the Barracks, along with the chaplain.' Paul listened to *Dragnet* on *AFN* and liked to use words like 'reckon'. But I couldn't figure out what 'the brass' was.

'What's 'the brass'?' Art Folan asked, as if reading my mind.

Paul looked at him from under heavily-lidded eyes. 'The top dogs,' he said, but then, seeing that Art and the rest of us still looked mystified, he added: 'You know, the OC and maybe the Adjutant and probably Father Whelan as well.'

We nodded in comprehension. Everybody knew that the OC was the highest officer in the Barracks, Colonel Austin. The Adjutant was less clear, but he was also an officer, and Father Whelan was the same as an officer, because he was a priest and he lived in the Officers' Mess.

We were stretched out in our usual places in the long back-seat of the green bus that had recently begun to serve as a link between the Barracks and the town. The bus was pulled up on the Barracks bridge, directly outside the front gate of the Barracks. Under the bridge ran the railroad: its steel rails curved eastwards to our right on to Athlone and Dublin; on our left, the railway speared its way along the coastline towards the town, hardly a mile away.

The bell rang, and the bus lumbered slowly away from the stop. I looked along the railway line but this morning there was nobody running frantically from the farm cottages that clung to the shore-line beyond the Barracks. Kathleen Cullen and the Gilmore girls who sold milk from silver cans in the Barracks had arrived on time today, and were seated up front with Miriam and the other girls. Missing the bus was a serious business: you had to rush down the Line to town, knowing that you were going to be late for school and pretty certain that, if the Brother was not in a good humour, you were going to get two from the cane on each palm. So far it hadn't happened to me.

Our first stop was well past the chapel, halfway along the military road. Only one passenger got on here, an older boy who lived in a two-storey farmhouse beside the bus-stop. At the next stop, at the corner of the Dublin Road, two boys got on the bus along with their two sisters, all from the little shop that stood beside the bus-stop. We viewed these new arrivals with not a little wariness. All of them were 'civvies', totally unaware of the unique world that existed within the walls of the Barracks. They were ignorant of the secrets of the Arch and the bullet that lodged in Paul O'Dowd's father's chin and how Number 2 and all the other Quarters were even now being given final polishings in readiness for the great inspection.

We picked up more civvies at the big crossroads on the Dublin Road, and the bus groaned upwards along the ascent beside the new cemetery. We examined with our usual pity the brother and sister who stood waiting at the stop outside the graveyard gates, condemned as they were to live and sleep in the forbidding lodge surrounded by creepy graves that their father tended as caretaker. Down the hill then, pausing to collect boys and girls as noisy as ourselves from the Corporation estate of Bohermore.

As we neared our stop on the Square in the town, we seemed to draw closer together, those of us from the Barracks, as if in closing ranks we could preserve our uniqueness, our other-worldliness. And anyway, it was our bus; everybody knew it was the Barracks bus, even though nobody stopped civvies getting on at any of the stops between the Barracks and the town.

As the bus lurched down the hill towards the Square, Art said: 'I'm staying in school today at dinner-hour because of the inspection.'

The rest of us chorused our agreement. Today we would not make the bus-trip out to the Barracks at dinner-hour to gulp down the usual meal, for the obvious reason that the Quarters had to be maintained throughout the day in complete inspection-worthy condition. Sandwiches of bread and butter and jam, eaten in the schoolyard, would be the order of the day; the spuds would be eaten in the evening when the inspection had been completed.

Only Paul O'Dowd demurred. 'Mother says I have to go home for a proper meal at mid-day,' he said.

I looked at Paul with sympathy. It all came from having no brothers or sisters, this calling your mammy 'Mother' and having to be different in so many other ways as well.

'I wonder,' said Art to nobody in particular, 'if they used to have inspections for the cavalry in the forts?'

'Not a chance,' Tommy McDonagh said.

'Why not?' Art asked. 'They had officers in the cavalry too.'

This was sound logic, and we looked to Tommy for an answer. Tommy had thick, black curly hair, probably because his father was the Barracks barber. 'Sure they wouldn't have time for inspections,' Tommy said, 'because they were always fighting off Injun attacks.'

This, too, was impeccable logic and Art nodded his agreement. 'I reckon you're right,' he said, 'the brass would have other things on their minds in the forts.' Art's words echoed Paul's in the manner in which we all fed off one another's vocabulary and knowledge.

There was so much to learn and discover, in the Barracks and in the town, and every day was a journey of yet more exploration.

We pushed our way off the bus, heedless of Hysey's appeals for an orderly exit from 'his bus', and hurried along the early-morning streets to our school. This morning I paid little attention to the shop-windows and the treasures they displayed; my mind was at home in Number 2, preparing for the inspection.

The day in Brother Edmond's class dragged on to its conclusion with all the agonising slowness of an arrow-stuck settler crawling on the sun-baked earth towards the sanctuary of the fort. Lunch-hour was a ridge in the distance: we inched upward along its slope, peering cautiously over it, through the mirage of the sixty-minute break spent in the narrow schoolyard, and trooped back disconsolately to our two-seater wooden desks for the last stretch of the day. We slithered through the undergrowth of English writing, hesitated and fumbled amid the jagged rocks of spelling, stumbled at last into the pastures of English reading. The fort was in sight. I felt Art's fingers pushing into my back. 'Ask Tony what time it is,' came his whispered instruction. We had no Western sun in the sky by which to measure the slow progress of the afternoon, only the watch on the wrist of Tony Smith, a quietly spoken 'civvie' who sat in the desk to my left.

I lifted my head cautiously from my book. Brother Edmond was standing in the aisle between the rows of desks just ahead, but with his back turned to me. I watched him bend his long frame forward, his finger jabbing at the words in Michael Long's book, as Michael read haltingly aloud. Very carefully – for Brother Edmond viewed inattentiveness with the same wrathful distaste as Kit Carson viewed thievin' Injuns – I reached out my left hand across the aisle to touch the sleeve of Tony's jumper. Tony was plump and sleek: he lifted his head slowly, like a dozy whale reluctantly waking in warm waters.

The silence of the classroom whispered around us, disturbed only by Michael's hesitant reading. 'Under – ' Michael halted, stumbling against the next syllable on the page. 'Under – ' he repeated.

Brother Edmond's finger jabbed harder on the page over which Michael was so painfully bent. With an abrupt movement Brother Edmond straightened himself; there was a swishing noise as he tugged characteristically at the wide green sash which belted his midriff and hung down against the left side of his black soutane. The sudden movement froze me, my arm stretched rigid across the aisle, fingers lock-jawed against Tony's sleeve. If Brother Edmond should turn around now, truly all was lost and the hooked bamboo cane would whistle through the air upon my palm. Open-mouthed horror settled on Tony's comfortable face as he too contemplated the inevitable punishment for felonious activity during class.

'Spell it,' Brother Edmond said quietly.

'U-N-D-E-R-' Michael began.

'Is "under",' Brother Edmond cut in. 'We know that you know that!' His voice rose. 'So will you please spell out the bit that you don't know!'

I hastily drew my arm back across the aisle to the safety of my own desk.

'N-E-A-T-H.' Michael's voice sounded deeper; his head was bent closer to the book as if he could discover knowledge or perhaps sanctuary by burying his head in the desk.

'Well?' the Brother's voice rose impatiently.

'Ne-Nay-' Michael floundered hopelessly.

Brother Edmond swung round to face the rest of the class. Anger had deepened the colour of his face to a dangerously rich shade of red. 'Hands up,' Brother Edmond said.

My hand was among those that shot into the air. Brother Edmond surveyed the sea of hands carefully. Sometimes he chose to demand the answer of somebody whose hand wasn't raised, although the sense of this always escaped me: what was the point, I wondered, of asking somebody who was letting you know that he didn't know the answer? There was no penalty, however, for not knowing the answer if your hand remained on the desk, but the hooked cane swished with extra venom onto any palm which was discovered to have been raised in an attempt to feign knowledge.

Brother Edmond's silent survey continued while Michael stumbled through a further litany of 'nays' and 'neats'. He laid an imperious hand on Michael's shoulder. 'That'll do,' he said. 'You.' He pointed at Art in the desk behind me, 'Art, c'mon, tell him what the word is.'

'Underneath, Brother,' Art bellowed in his powerful voice. 'U-N-D-E-R-N-E-A-T-H, underneath.'

Brother Edmond nodded. 'Good man,' he said. He turned his back to us again, jabbing at Michael's book.

While Michael limped on at the reading, Tony held up his left wrist so that Art and I could read the time from his watch. Not much more than five minutes to go to half past three. The gates of the fort were in sight.

While I and the other Barracks-boys day-dreamed about the inspection at home and the officers parading their proud shoes and soft uniforms about the rooms of our Married Quarters, Michael's voice scrambled towards the end of the page, and safe haven was reached for another day, and the bell was heard ringing outside, but nobody closed books or reached for school-bags, because to do so was also felonious until Brother Edmond had personally nodded his intimation of the end of another day at school. His nod was not delayed today, and we stood quietly, and lifted the seats of our desks on their squeaky iron hinges, and we buckled our school-bags shut, and we blessed ourselves in unison, and recited together, in Irish, one Our Father and three Hail Mary's and one Glory Be To The Father, and added the Hail Holy Queen in English, and we blessed ourselves again, and we forced ourselves to file silently and slowly from the classroom, (even when you thought you were safe you could still be called back), and we said goodbye to Brother Edmond as we passed him at his desk (for most of us liked him well enough, even though he got cross sometimes), and then finally we were free, and haring along the lane that spilled us out onto the streets of the town, and we were racing towards the station and the Line, and hoping and praying that the inspection of the Married Quarters might not be over.

It wasn't.

Big Bartley, the PA on duty, laid a large restraining hand across my path as I attempted to dash through the gate into the barracks.

'Where d'you think you're off to?' Bartley growled. His round face was as red as the distinctive peak on his military policeman's cap: he always remined me of Biffo the Bear in the *Beano*, although Biffo didn't seem to be as cross as Bartley. Trying to push my way past Bartley was futile: he simply spread his sausage fingers wider and laid them against my chest like a five-barred gate. 'Ye're not thinkin'of rushin' in home just now, are ye?' Bartley demanded.

Art pushed himself forward beside me. Behind us Tommy McDonagh and Bobby Dunne crowded into the small space of the Gate. Our faces were as red as Bartley's from the exertion of running at full tilt along the Line. 'We're after breaking the record for running the Line,' Art said, 'so that we'd be in time for the inspection.' Only Paul O'Dowd had declined to join our headlong rush from town: his mother had advised him against running and so getting himself unhealthily covered in perspiration.

Bartley's eyes glinted at our steaming faces from beneath his red peak. 'Ye can't,' he said. 'Ye can't see the inspection.'

Instinctively we howled in united protest.

'Childer,' said Bartley, hooking his right thumb into the breast pocket of his tunic, 'are not allowed at a Married Quarters inspection.'

Art ignored the PA. He half-turned to address Tommy, Bobby and myself. 'It sounds,' Art said to us, 'as if the inspection isn't over anyway.'

'If the inspection was over,' Bartley announced with ponderous logic, 'I wouldn't be keepin' ye here to prevent ye from interferin' with the inspection.'

'How far have they got around the Quarters?' Tommy McDonagh asked. Tommy would ask crucial questions with the utmost innocence, his eyes focused somewhere over your shoulder to convey his complete lack of interest in the answer.

Bartley flexed his tunic-clad shoulders and then adjusted his red-peaked cap. His knowledge added to his stature. 'In fact,' he said, looking at me, 'the CO and the rest of them went into Number 2 only a minute before ye got here – I saw them myself from this very spot. They're workin' the inspection backwards, so they have only Number 1 left to do after this.'

'That's my house!' Art exclaimed.

'So it is,' Bartley said, 'and you're far better off waitin' here than to be in at home annoyin' your mother when the CO is inside doin' the inspection.

'But they're in my house now!' I exploded. 'I want to see them!'

'Your Mammy,' Bartley said, 'will thank me for keepin' you here out of her way.'

'It's not fair!' I shouted, pushing uselessly against his beefy left hand.

'No, it's not fair!' Tommy and Art cried out together. The three of us moved towards the exit into the Barracks. A hundred yards away I could see the high kitchen windows of Number 2 sparkling in the afternoon sunlight.

Bartley unhooked his right hand from his tunic pocket and spread his arms to bar our passage. 'I warned ye,' he growled, his face reddening even more.

Tommy, Art and I advanced slowly towards the door. Out of the corner of my eye I noticed that Bobby Dunne was holding back.

'Somebody is after shittin' on the floor.'

All of us, including Bartley, froze at Bobby's words. We twisted to look at Bobby. He was crouched over the floor of the Gate, his back turned towards us.

'What did you say?' Bartley's voice boomed in the confined space.

'Someone,' Bobby said, still not turning to face us, 'is after shittin' all over the floor here.' His voice seemed to come from between his short legs, white above the grey socks that reached to his knees.

'Who's after shittin' where in my gate?' Bartley roared. 'What kinda bullshit are you talkin' at all?' He pushed us brusquely aside and moved towards Bobby, half crouched inside the front door of the gate.

Bobby suddenly straightened and nimbly side-stepped Bartley. 'Run!' he yelled, his eyes dancing in their sockets. We needed no further exhortation. Bartley's beefy paw clutched only at the air as Bobby, small and light-of-foot, sped by him.

Jubilant with our escape, we raced into the Barracks, our school-bags pounding on our backs. Behind us, Bartley bellowed in fury.

'One for all!' Bobby shouted as we ran in the shadow of the Barracks wall towards our homes.

'And all for one!' the rest of us yelled. Paul O'Dowd had introduced a Classics comic of *The Three Musketeers* into our Barracks lending circle just a week previously, and D'Artagnan and his companions sometimes supplanted the heroes of the Wild West in our over-heated imaginations.

'Paul will get the works,' Art panted, 'when he's coming through.'

'Arra, he won't,' said Bobby, 'isn't his father a PA.' The knowledge made us all feel relieved, as we hurtled towards the Quarters. Paul's only-child condition had made him undeniably different from the rest of us, but he was entitled to the protection of membership.

Clenched fists triumphantly smiting the air, we paused for breath at the top of the short flight of stone steps that led down to the Married Quarters.

'Farewell, my brothers-in-arms,' Art said. 'Here we come to the parting of the ways.' Art, alone among us, would not be descending the steps; the way to Number 1 was straight on past the gable-end of the Married Quarters.

'I hope that Bartley isn't on the Gate when we're going to school tomorrow,' Tommy said, but the twinkle in his eyes belied the caution of his words.

'I hope he's not on the Gate for the next year,' I said. Bartley's temper was well known. His threats to lodge 'bold boys' in the guard-room, the unseen prison for soldiers in custody, were always uttered with furious conviction.

'All the same,' Art said, 'it was a great plot, Bobby. How did you think of it?'

'Yeah,' said Tommy. 'Shit on the floor – how did you think of it?'

Bobby spoke deadpan: 'I just wanted to throw Bartley off the scent.' We broke up with laughter, the inspection, for these laughing moments, far from our thoughts.

'And then,' I blurted out, 'he asked why you were talking bullshit!'

Once more we dissolved into tears of laughter. Over to our right, facing Number 2, the armourer, Mick Sheehan, was working at the door of his workshop, and I hoped he could not hear the bad words we were bandying about. My mother's wrath would be no less than Bartley's, if she heard that I was using bad language. Mick, however, paid no attention to us; the rifle that he held against his grease-stiffened black overalls was the centre of all his attention. Or so it seemed, until Mick lowered his rifle, propping it against the metal half-door of the armourer's workshop. We watched him as he approached us. There was a smudge of rifle-grease on the front of his brylcreemed hair.

'Lads,' he said quietly when he stood beside us, 'd'ye not know that the CO and the other officers are inside Number 2 at this very minute?'

We could not meet his gaze, looking sheepishly at one another. 'Yes,' I said, 'we know.'

'Well, don't you think ye should be a bit quieter then? Sure the way ye're goin' on, ye could be heard at the foot of the Line.' We mumbled our agreement, still not looking at Mick. He made as if to go back to his workshop, but then stopped and came close to us again. 'Are you goin' in home now, Kevin?' he asked me.

'Yes,' I said.

Mick looked thoughtful. 'Well, go in if you like,' he said, 'but be quiet about it, and don't get in the way. It isn't every day you'll have the CO in your house. Right?'

I nodded, and Mick gave me a thoughtful look before going back to his workshop.

The other lads looked graver now. Mick's quietly delivered words had impressed upon us far more forcefully than Bartley's bluster the enormity of the drama being enacted at this very moment in Number 2. The CO was inspecting my home. Very soon the drama would be re-enacted in Number 1.

'One for all,' I said quietly. I held my right hand out in front of me, palm down.

Tommy, Art and Bobby laid their hands in a pyramid on top of mine. 'And all for one,' they said together. For a few seconds we left our hands there, a bond forged as much in the hot-house of our imaginations as in the grey confines of the Barracks.

'We'll meet at the Arch,' Art said, 'when the inspection is all over.' He half-waved and then trotted away around the gable-end to Number 1. The rest of us went down the stone steps, silent now as we passed by the tall, shining windows of our kitchen. My mother had hung new net-curtains across the lower half of the windows and it was impossible to see anything through them. Bobby and Tommy left me quietly, and I stood alone on the doorstep of Number 2.

I looked over my shoulder at the upturned soles of my boots before stepping inside: my mother had scrubbed the stone hallway the previous night, working her way back up the hall on her knees, rhythmically scrubbing with the hard brush, dragging the tin bucket of darkening sudsy water as she moved slowly backwards. She'd rested a couple of times during the work, still on her knees, her bottom settled on her heels while she surveyed the slick and shining dark-grey floor of stone.

My boots seemed free of dirt, but I scraped them anyway on the iron shoe-scraper set into the door-step. Her face had been drenched with sweat when she'd finished, wet as the long, stone hall that shone from her exertions. I remembered how her shoulders sagged as she'd emptied the bucket of dirty water down the big sink in the scullery, and I turned each boot sideways against the metal scraper, just to make extra sure.

I pushed the hall door open quietly. Even the green-distempered walls gleamed from her cleaning with a soft cloth. Minute silvery shards glinted in the stone floor. I moved my boot-shod feet with exaggerated caution on the hard surface. Voices came indistinctly from the kitchen. The door from the hall to the scullery was very slightly ajar, and I leaned against the jamb, straining to make out what was being said. It was useless; the inside door, leading from the scullery into the kitchen, was closed.

The deep rumble of a strange, masculine voice alternated with my mother's higher-pitched tones. I wanted fiercely to know what she was saying to the CO, what he was saying to her. She'd be standing there in the middle of the shining kitchen, and Colonel Austin and the chaplain and the other officer, the adjutant, would be admiring the black-and-silver range that she'd blacked with black-lead and polished with silver polish, and they'd marvel at the way she'd pinned my father's hurling medals on to the black velvet shield, and they'd be as full of wonder as I was at the way she'd stood the shield on top of the chest of drawers, surrounded by framed photographs of my father in various team-groups. They'd see the golden handles gleaming with Brasso on the drawers, and the crisp curtains tied neatly with the new ribbons, and they'd know – these officers in soft tunics – they'd know, as I knew, that there was no mother in the world like mine.

I longed to be in the kitchen, to witness my mother's triumph, but I was terrified at the thought of opening the door. Art and the lads would be gathering at the Arch: an attack on the encampment of renegade redskins at the river's bend might be in preparation.

I turned to leave, turned back again. I felt the perspiration on my forehead and was ashamed of my own fear.

I stepped resolutely into the scullery and put my hand on the brass knob of the kitchen door. Once more my frightened heart fluttered against my ribs.

'Kevin?' I heard my mother's voice call my name from within the kitchen. The murmur of the other voices ceased. 'Kevin? Is that you?' Again she called out to me, and then the knob was turned from the other side, and the door swung inwards, and my mother stood smiling down at me, while Colonel Austin and the others stood watching. She drew me to her side, her hand resting on my shoulder.

'Is this the eldest lad?' Colonel Austin asked. He was a short man with a kind face. His Sam Browne could not contain his protruding midriff.

'This is Kevin, sir,' my mother said.

'He looks old enough to be making his First Holy Communion,' Father Whelan said. The chaplain looked infinitely nobler than the colonel. When he smiled you could see his even white teeth, and his officer's uniform hung neatly on him. His priest's collar shone white as his teeth inside the dark-green tunic.

'He'll be making his First Communion this year, please God,' my mother said. 'He's six now.' I fidgeted under her hand and she added quickly: 'Well, he'll be seven in a few months.' I wondered if the officers could hear the latent laughter in her voice.

'Maybe he'd like to come and serve Mass then,' the priest said, and there was a question in his voice.

'Would you like to serve Mass?' I felt my mother's touch tighten on my shoulder as she repeated the question.

I wanted to answer yes, but the words caught in my throat as I looked at the men who stood waiting for my answer in our kitchen. Their peaked caps rested on the chest of drawers beside the shield of medals, and you could see the rich leather trim that lined the inside of the caps. Their uniforms were fine and soft, unlike the hard bull's-wool material that made up the uniforms of my father and the other men. My father wore blood-red boots and short leggings that reached up over his calves, but those men wore dark-brown shoes that gleamed softly against the falling folds of their dark-green trousers.

I managed to croak an answer that yes, I'd like to be a server at Mass, and my mother's fingers pressed briefly into my shoulder, and the chaplain smiled again and his teeth gleamed like fresh snow, and the colonel harrumphed and said that that was very good. Where were the other children, he wanted to know.

Mrs Lally was keeping an eye on them, my mother told him, until the inspection was over – the colonel nodded understandingly – and sure hadn't they seen the baby asleep when they inspected the bedroom?

'A beautiful baby,' the colonel said, and my mother said thank you. The chaplain smiled again. The third officer, standing beside the colonel, neither smiled nor spoke. He was a tall, stringy man with a long neck and a pinched face. I wondered if adjutants weren't allowed to speak in the presence of a colonel, like ourselves and Brother Edmond.

'And your home is not only beautiful,' the colonel added. 'It's a credit to you, Mrs Brophy.'

'Thank you, sir,' my mother said, and her voice wobbled with delight.

'The repairs that need doing have been noted, haven't they?' the colonel said.

It was when he half-turned that I saw the fourth man, a short fellow in civilian clothes and a brown hat. He jabbed with his pen at the hard-backed notebook he held in his hand. 'It's all written down,' he said, 'I've got it all here.'

I knew Mick O'Toole to see around the Barracks; he was the fore-man of the civilian tradesmen and labourers who did the maintenance work. As civvies they did not rank at all in our military hierarchy; we knew them simply and collectively as 'the workmen', regardless of whether they pushed wheelbarrows or used the tools of craftsmen.

'You won't forget the light in the far scullery?' I was surprised by the oddly apologetic note in my mother's voice. 'It's been broken for ages.'

Mick O'Toole jabbed again at his notebook. 'I've made a note,' he said, somewhat testily.

The colonel looked at him and said mildly: 'Please see that that particular job is done first thing tomorrow.'

The foreman's Adam's apple bobbed in his throat as he swal-lowed. This time he jabbed at the brim of his hat with his pen. 'First thing,' he said, 'in the morning.'

I looked up at my mother and saw the small smile on her mouth. 'Thank you, sir,' she said again.

'For nothing at all, ma'am,' Colonel Huston said to her. 'We've taken up far too much of your time, and you with a home to run and children to feed.'

My mother said nothing. The chaplain smiled again. The adjutant looked bored. Mick O'Toole fidgeted with his pen.

The colonel shook hands with my mother, and then extended his hand towards me. His fingers were soft and warm, his nails cut short and scrubbed white. 'Thank you,' he said to me. I blushed, unable to speak, and he took his hand from mine, and I felt his fingers briefly touch my face.

They picked up their caps from the chest of drawers and moved towards the door. My mother led them across the scullery and into the long hall, and I could hear the last exchanges of thanks and farewells coming from the front door.

I stood motionless in the kitchen, my school-bag still strapped on my back, and I heard my mother's footsteps coming back up the hall. Her face was shining as she came into the kitchen. 'They're going to fix that light in the scullery tomorrow,' she said to me.

I unbuckled my school-bag and laid it on the floor. 'I don't care about the old light,' I said.

'I know,' she said, and she was smiling.

'The CO said it was a beautiful home, Mammy,' I said to her.

'I know,' she said, and her smile was brighter now.

'He's dead right,' I said to her. 'I wish there was a prize for the best Quarters – I know you'd have got it.'

She put her two hands on my shoulders and held me at arm's length. 'There's no need for prizes,' she said earnestly, 'if you're doing your best.'

There were times when women, even including my mother, didn't appreciate the necessity to do battle and win. But I didn't say that to her, not now in her shining moment. 'I bet you'd have won it anyway,' was all I said to her.

FIVE

I buttered the heel of the loaf carefully and then spread a thick coating of mixed fruit jam on top of the layer of butter. Miriam, seated on my left, was waiting for the jam and I pushed the big two-pound pot across in front of her. My father sat opposite me at the other end of the kitchen table. The *Irish Press* lay on the table beside him, folded open at the racing page. A sharp-pointed yellow pencil waited in readiness beside the lists of horses and riders.

Nobody spoke at the tea-time table. Even Jacky, usually the soul of loquacious nonsense, was silent while the BBC weather-forecaster intoned the meteorological prospects for Dogger Bank, Wash, Humber, and other locations of often-heard unreality. Jacky had wanted the heel of the loaf, although it hadn't been his turn, but my father had silenced his protests with a silent glare and a thump on the table with the folded newspaper. Now Jacky sat, wordless and nearly immobile at the inside of the table. Mammy was seated at the outside of the table, on my father's left. Danny, nearly two years old, sat blubbering on her lap, although Mammy made sure that none of his dribbles landed on the folded racing page. Baby Martha was asleep in the bedroom.

I delayed before biting into the heel. The end of the loaf had a special flavour all of its own, the soft flesh of the shop bread melting in your mouth as your teeth tore away at the crusty exterior. If you arranged the crust like a diamond across a square of the creamy oil-cloth, then you could make an eight-pointed sheriff's star out of the resulting combination. The stars pinned to the chests of sheriffs and marshals were confusing, however: some of them were eight-pointed, like my crust-and-square arrangement, whereas others were sunburst circles, surrounded by a pattern of points. I'd have to check with Paul O'Dowd about the significance of the two kinds of star.

71

I picked up my heel-star and bit into it. Butter and jam blended deliciously in my mouth with hard crust and fleshy dough. Jacky caught my eye and I wrinkled up my nose at him, chewing ostentatiously. He took care to cover his mouth with his hand, so that my father would not see him sticking his tongue out at me.

Danny bounced on Mammy's lap. He spluttered on a mouthful of goody – a concoction of white bread and sugar, mixed in an enamel army mug with milk and hot water – and Mammy wiped his mouth and chin with the towel that she kept on her lap. My father paused briefly from eating the round steak that Mammy had fried on the range, but made no comment.

'I met that woman, Mrs Wakeling, when I was out the road to the shop today.' My mother's quietly spoken words sounded loud over the silent table. My father went on eating. The BBC voice droned nasally on from the wireless behind my father.

'Who's Mrs Wakeling?' I asked.

'The new lady who moved in out the road, into the house near the bus-stop, you know the one.' Mammy looked at my father, but he showed no interest in Mrs Wakeling.

'They have a motor car,' I said.

'You know them?' Mammy asked, carefully loading another spoonful of goody into Danny's mouth.

'I see them sometimes when the bus is passing by,' I said to her. 'They have a motor car,' I repeated.

'I know.'

'And they're Protestants,' I added in a whisper.

My father's chair scraped on the kitchen floor as he pushed back from the table. He half-turned in the chair, reaching out to turn up the volume on the wireless. A new BBC voice had taken over from the weather-forecaster. 'And we begin our sports report with today's racing results. First, the results from Pontefract . . .'

My father had his pencil and paper ready. Nobody at the table stirred while he marked the winners on the *Irish Press*. He drew a stroke from the name of each winner and attached it to the figure 1 and then beside it wrote the odds of the winner. He also drew two short strokes from the names of the horses which came second and third. I wanted to ask him why he never bothered to add the figures 2 and 3 so that he'd know which was which: for some reason the order of these two places didn't seem to matter.

This evening I had no interest whatever in the reason for this. I wanted to hear about the Wakelings. They were Protestants. The older boy who lived in the farmhouse across the road had let this be known on the bus in grave undertones. None of us had ever met a Protestant, but we knew that they couldn't get into heaven when they died. And my mother had spoken to Mrs Wakeling today. *Wakeling.* It was like a name out of a book, not like Brophy or McDonagh or Folan. It wasn't a name you'd hear in the Barracks or in the town. Up to that moment I never knew that such a name existed. Would the results from Pontefract never end, so that Mammy could tell me more? They would but, horror of infuriating horrors, the BBC began yet another litany of results with the 2.15 from Folkestone.

Intermittently the static-laden voice broke down, and my father leaned closer to the crackling wireless. Concentration made his handsome face sterner even than usual; he moved the pencil across the page with firm, neat strokes that would have won Brother Edmond's approval. His tunic hung over the back of his chair; with his sleeves rolled up, and wearing the collarless shirt of rough grey stuff that all the soldiers wore, he seemed to me so muscular and powerful that no Saint Peter or sentinel angel could deny him entry to heaven or anywhere else.

Finally the wireless voice began to announce the result of the 4.45 at Folkestone, the last of the races. When it was done, my father reached out his hand and cut off the announcer in mid-sentence as he moved on to the day's cricket scores. Cricket was a Protestant game; so was soccer. Catholics played hurling and Gaelic football. Tennis seemed vaguely Protestant too, but it was confusing because the officers played it on the lawn.

'Any good?' my mother asked.

My father went on examining the results he had marked on the paper for some time. 'Only one up,' he said at last, 'two of them let me down.'

I felt sorry for these two unsuccessful horses which had failed to win my father's approval by winning. I knew from watching him writing out his bets at lunch-hour that you picked three horses to bet a treble and three cross-doubles. Having one winner was no good; at least two of your selections had to win before you clicked a double. If all three of your horses won – such a result had once occurred – then not only did you get three doubles up, but you had a winning treble as well.

Again my father's eyes scanned the page. 'Britt had a double,' he said aloud, 'And Elsey along with him.'

My mother went on with her ladling of the goody: she knew as much about horse-racing as did Danny, bouncing on her lap. Sometimes I looked at the paper after my father had finished with it. He put a horizontal mark across the trainer's name of any horse he backed. Such a mark did not often coincide with the figure 1 that showed a winner. And from my father's regretful tone, I guessed that he had not selected either of the horses that had given Britt a double. Britt, I knew from my own examination of the racing page, was a jockey; Elsey was a trainer. I had never heard of anybody in the town being called Britt or Elsey. Maybe all trainers and jockeys were Protestants, too. Like Mrs Wakeling.

'It's a queer name,' I said to my mother.

She could read my thoughts. 'Musha, it is,' she said. 'I never came across it before.'

My father laid the folded newspaper on the table beside his plate. 'What's a queer name?' he asked, looking up.

'Wakeling,' Mammy said. 'That's what I'm tellin' you – I met Mrs Wakeling today.'

Jacky chanted: 'Wakeling, Wakeling, the big fat breakling.' He could always be relied on to produce a few words of gibberish.

My father frowned. 'Never heard of any Wakelings,' he said. 'Are they civvies out the road?'

My mother nodded. 'They just moved in a month ago.'

'I didn't notice any strangers among the civvies at Mass,' he said. There was a note of accusation in his voice, as if the Wakelings might be deliberately hiding themselves among the few civilians who mixed with the soldiers at the Sunday Mass.

'They don't go to Mass,' I blurted out. 'They're Protestants.'

My father's level gaze moved from me to my mother. 'Are they?'

'They are,' Mammy said, and you could see that she was pleased to have my father's attention. 'I didn't say a word about it, mind, but she mentioned it herself, about the daughter going to the Protestant school in town.'

'What daughter?'

'They have one daughter,' Mammy said patiently, wiping

Danny's mouth with the towel and lowering him to the floor. 'She's an only child – they call her Rosemary, she's only a couple of years older than Kevin.'

Rosemary. Another name out of a book, a name to go with Wakeling. I felt my father's eyes upon me, as if he were measuring this Protestant Rosemary who was a couple of years older than me. I dropped my gaze to the squares on the oil-cloth.

'And what does himself do – this Mister Wakeling?'

'I think she said he's something in insurance,' Mammy said.

'You *think* she said?'

I noticed the pause before Mammy made answer. 'She *did* say that'.

'You got great information out of the woman altogether,' my father said slowly. 'You must have done nothing but ask her questions.'

'I asked her nothing,' my mother retorted, 'except how did she like livin' here. What else would you say to any woman who was just after movin' in?'

I kept my eyes on the table-cloth, studying the red roses with great attentiveness. I wished only that the bickering would stop. I wanted to ask my mother if Mrs Wakeling was frightened because she and Mr Wakeling, who did something in insurance, and their only child, Rosemary, who was a couple of years older than me, would not be admitted to heaven when they died. Why didn't my father stop getting at Mammy and just listen to her telling the story?

'I met her on my way out to the shop,' Mammy was saying. 'I was passing her house when she was turning in at her own gate. She had her messages on her bicycle, and I just held the gate open for her and we got talkin'.'

'I thought you said they had a motor car?' My father's tone was sharp.

'I suppose himself had the motor car gone to work,' Mammy said. 'Anyway I held the gate open for her and we had a good long chat.' My mother was silent for a little while, and then she added: 'She asked me in for a cuppa tea, but I didn't like to.'

I looked at Mammy in astonishment. 'She's a Protestant, Mammy,' I said, aghast.

My mother smiled at me. 'I'm sure the woman likes a cuppa tea like the rest of us,' she said to me.

'But they can't get to heaven,' I insisted. We had to learn it at school. *Outside the Church there is no salvation.* We spent extra time at school learning the Catechism: our First Communion Day was just over a month away. 'Outside the Church there is no salvation,' I recited gravely. 'That means you can't get to heaven if you're not a Catholic.'

My mother seemed unimpressed by the flourish with which I spoke.

'I'm sure I wouldn't know anything about that,' Mammy said. 'Sure wasn't the woman only talkin' about havin' a cuppa tea?'

'But – '

'There's no "buts", Kevin,' my mother said, 'and remember that she's a very nice lady.'

I blushed, discomfited, and resumed my examination of the rose on the oil-cloth.

'What did you say their name was?' I heard my father ask.

'Wakeling, she said.'

My father shook his head. 'We had plenty of Protestants down at home,' my father said, 'but we had no Wakelings among them.'

My ears pricked up. Before my father joined the army he had lived in another county called Kilkenny. He hardly ever spoke of it. 'Did you know any Proddies, Dad?' I asked him.

Jacky chanted: 'Proddy, proddy, the big, fat broddy . . .'

My father chuckled at this inane intervention, and mussed Jacky's hair with his fingers. He was my father's pet. 'I knew plenty of them,' he said to me. 'Didn't I work on their farms during the week and play cricket with them on Sundays?'

I was flabbergasted: my father, who played hurling on our county team, playing cricket with Protestants! 'I never knew you played cricket, Dad,' I said to him. 'What was it like?'

My father shrugged. 'It was like any game, maybe a bit boring when you were fielding, but it was okay when you were at the wicket and you had the bat.'

It was the longest speech my father had ever addressed directly to me. His words created in my mind an incongruous picture of comic-story characters clad in white flannels, shouting 'Howzat!' across the cricket pitches of English boarding-schools while boys in blazers and tiny school-caps bit their nails as the last man went in to bat, needing thirteen runs and the light fading around the ivy-clad quad and belfry; it was an image I could not reconcile with my father's rough grey shirt and his massive biceps and the *Irish Press* folded open in front of him on the table. There was so much more I wanted to know about him.

'Had you a bat, Dad, and pads and gloves and all the rest of the stuff they use?'

Jacky started another of his mindless chants, but my mother hushed him: in her own stillness I sensed her attentiveness to this exchange between my father and myself.

'They had all that gear up in Scott's house,' my father said. 'The bat and the ball and the stumps and all the rest of it.' He was thoughtful for a moment, frowning with the effort of remembering. 'I don't remember any gloves though – I took a belt off that ball across my knuckles more than once and I can tell you it hurt a lot more than a clout from any *sliotar*.'

Sliotar was the Irish word for hurling ball: Brother Edmond had taught us how to spell it. Up to then I had thought it to be just another English word, because all the lads used it anyway.

'And had ye a stand and all, and seats, and a scoreboard an' everything?' There was so much I needed to know!

My father rarely laughed out loud like Mammy. Instead he just smiled with his lips, as he did now, looking at me along the length of the table. 'Stands and scoreboards!' he scoffed, but there was no hardness in his tone. 'God help your head! Mister Scott kept the big field in front of the house trimmed for the matches in the season, but you'd still have to watch out for the cow-dung in the out-field.'

'Cow-dung?'

'He let the cows into the field during the week, but he made sure that the wicket was roped off so that the cows couldn't get onto it. It wouldn't do to have a nice heap of cow-dung right in front of the wicket when the vicar was coming in to bat, would it?'

'The vicar?' I wasn't sure if I was hearing correctly. 'Ye had a Protestant minister on the team?'

The table was quiet: Miriam and my mother were listening as carefully as I was – even Jacky seemed to have given up, temporarily anyway, on the improvisation of further inane chants.

'Sure of course the minister was on the team – wasn't it the parish team?' My father must have noticed the look of puzzlement on my face for he went on to explain: 'The Protestant parish – they had their parish and we had ours, or Father Delaney had it, and the two parishes covered nearly the same ground, although they hadn't nearly as many people as ourselves. Sure isn't that why they'd draft in a few of us to play for them on a Sunday when they were playing a different club or another parish?'

My mind whirled in confusion. In that far-off county called Kilkenny my father swung the willow bat with deadly accuracy and thumped the hard ball through the dung-splattered out-field while the Protestant minister looked on approvingly and the Sunday evening countryside echoed with the applause of men and women and children who must go to hell when they died.

'And the priest – Father Delaney – did he not mind?' My question was fractured and uncertain.

'Mind what?'

'Did he not mind ye playing with the Protestants and the minister and all?'

'Sure what'd be wrong with playing with them?' I quailed before my father's indignation. 'And what'd be wrong with the vicar? Reverend Ireland was the best bat on the side anyway. And sure he never said much to any of us except "Thank you, chaps" and "Well done, chaps".'

'But at school we learned – I mean – outside the Church . . .'

My father's indignation turned to impatience. 'You don't want to believe half that oul' stuff,' he said angrily. Abruptly he pushed back his chair and stood up. 'Don't they put their trousers on one leg at a time like the rest of us?'

Before his hard words and steely gaze I dropped my eyes. Nobody spoke as he moved to the kitchen door and into the scullery. We heard the bolt being pushed home in the lavatory. I felt tears stinging at my eyes. 'Why does Dad have to get cross?' I asked my mother.

She reached out and laid her hand on mine on top of the table. 'He's not really cross,' she said. 'It's just his way.'

I sniffled, and my fingers tightened around hers.

'Cry-baby! Cry-baby!' Jacky managed to stick his tongue out at me in between chants.

My mother silenced him with an admonitory finger. 'It's only his way,' she said again.

I gulped down the incipient sobs. 'I just don't understand,' I said. 'I mean – '

'Hush!' my mother soothed. 'Don't be botherin' yourself about things like that. Now,' she went on more brightly, 'didn't you like listenin' to your Dad talkin' about the cricket and his own place and all that?'

Words without gulping tears still seemed too much, so I merely nodded. Kilkenny was remote and mysterious, at the furthest ends of the shining railroad that snaked its way across the land outside the Barracks gate. My father's words, with their glimpse of his own life in the distant past, made it even more remote, more mysterious. Maybe they played cricket over there with the Reverend Ireland and all the others so that they could convert them, like the missionaries did with the black babies in Africa, and then they'd all be saved and they could go to heaven.

'Won't you talk to your Daddy again?' my mother asked me.

Again I nodded. 'What did he mean,' I asked her, 'about them putting their trousers on one leg at a time like the rest of us?'

'It's only a way of saying that they're the same as the rest of us. D'you see?'

I did see. It was a good saying and could be used to impress Paul O'Dowd at some later date.

'Trousers, trousers, the big fat lousers!' Jacky was at it again. My mother looked from him to me and we both burst out laughing.

'Kevin!'

My mother's soft whisper seemed part of a dream. Through the veil of awakening eyes her face softened into focus, close to mine. The soapy smell of her, clean and fresh, cut through the odorous warmth of the bed, rousing me further from sleep. Her hand was on my shoulder, shaking me gently, and I could feel the morning coldness of her fingers through the fabric of the grey army shirt that I wore in bed.

I started to speak, but she laid her fingers across my lips. 'Don't waken the others,' she whispered.

I was lying on my side, my back turned to Jacky and Miriam, both still sleeping behind me in the double bed. I rubbed my knuckles against my eyes and felt the yellow crust of sleep crumble away on my fingers. My mother had not turned the light on, nor had she opened the curtains that were drawn across the tall, narrow window of the bedroom, but I could still see, in the grey light of the morning, that Mammy was already dressed in her best navy skirt and jumper.

It came back to me then, that this was the day of my First Holy Communion.

Mammy turned back the corner of the grey blankets and I swung my legs out. The army shirt had ridden up over my bottom while I slept and I pulled it down to cover myself. 'Get yourself dressed quickly and come on out to the kitchen,' she said, 'and make sure you don't waken the others.' Her fingers touched my hair and then she tiptoed out of the room on bare feet.

It took a few moments for my own bare feet to adjust to the cold sting of the linoleum. This morning, however, there could be no histrionic exclamations of pain as I barefooted it across the frozen wastes of Alaska, desperately inching my starving way to the cache of supplies in the shack on top of the mountain . . . Jacky stirred in his sleep, his arm jerked across Miriam's pale face, framed in her sleep-sticky hair, and she drew away from him without waking, her breathing raspy in the half-lighted room.

I was glad that they were still asleep. My lips moved as I prayed to Jesus that Danny and Martha might also remain asleep, in the other room.

On this morning of all mornings it would be good to have Mammy and the kitchen to myself.

My Communion suit waited for me on the kitchen chair against the wall. The jacket was draped across the back of the chair, the trousers folded on top of the jacket. I lifted the short trousers in my hands and touched the navy-blue fabric with reverence. They were the first trousers I had ever owned that Mammy had not made for me on the table in the kitchen; they were redolent of all the riches of the Blackrock shop in the main street in town. I drew them on and marvelled at the snugness of their fit, the freshness of the cloth on my skin.

I pulled off my night-shirt and picked up the half-sleeved vest that Mammy had also bought for me. Next came the new white shirt. I had removed the pins and stiffening board and opened all the buttons the night before, and it now lay in starched readiness on the seat of the chair. The white cloth was crisp in my hands;

the cuffs folded around my wrists like D'Artagnan's ruffles. When I tucked the shirt inside my pants, its long tail wrapped around my bottom like a fresh, cool skin. I buttoned up the fly of my trousers and fastened the shiny silver clasp in the middle of the waist-band.

My new white ankle-socks poked out from the mouth of the black patent-leather shoes that gleamed on the linoleum beside the chair. I sat on the chair and pulled on the socks, turning them down over my ankles so that you could see the thin blue lines that decorated their tops. I stood up and collected my jacket from the back of the chair, then bent to pick up my shoes. With my hands full I tip-toed from the bedroom.

My mother already had the fire lighting in the range. The heat filled the kitchen; blue flames darted like tongues between the bars of the grate.

'It's lovely and warm in here, Mammy,' I said.

'It's hard to believe it's June,' she said to me. She was setting out the mug and the plate and the knife for my father at the head of the table. The bread and butter and sugar and milk lay ready on the table before his place. 'I just want to leave everything ready for your Daddy.' She was adjusting the positions of the sugar bowl and the milk jug as she spoke. 'I'll give the others something to eat when we get back.' Her wide eyes grew serious. 'When we get back, you'll be different,' she said to me. 'You know that?'

I nodded. Brother Edmond had drummed it all into us so often that I could recite it all by heart, even in my sleep. *This is My Body. This is My Blood.*

'It's a very, very special day for you.'

'Yes,' I said. *Corpus Christi. Amen.*

Once more she busied herself at the table. The glow from the fire reached to her bent head and cast a lustrous sheen on her long black hair.

'Mammy?'

'What is it, *a ghrá*?' She spoke without looking up from her work.

'It's nice with just the two of us in the kitchen, isn't it?'

She looked up then from the table. For a moment her eyes clouded.

She came round the table and knelt beside me. 'It *is* nice,' she said. 'Sometimes I think I don't talk to you enough anymore, but I have to look after all the young ones as well and – and you're growing up now anyway, you're going to receive your First Holy Communion today.' She held my face in both her hands and drew me closer to her. 'You do understand, don't you?'

She didn't let me answer her question but hugged me even more closely to her. In the silence of the kitchen I could hear the thumping of our hearts, louder than the ticking of the alarm-clock on the mantelpiece.

When she drew back from me, she said again: 'You'll be different when we come back home from the church.'

I nodded. My cheek felt wet where her face had rested against mine. She busied herself then, making sure that I was properly dressed. She held my jacket for me and I slipped my arms into sleeves that were rich with satiny lining. It took a couple of minutes before the collar of my white shirt was arranged to her satisfaction, draped out over the collar of my jacket. I had modelled the suit and shiny shoes for her before, both in the shop and at home, but she made me parade again across the kitchen, and stand there by the door into the scullery until she had assured herself that everything was in order. I needed no second prompting. I stood like a king in my new outfit and grew taller in the warmth of her praise.

'The navy looks grand on you,' she said finally, 'and the double-breasted suits you well.'

She mixed a little of my father's Brylcreem into my hair, freshly cut by Tommy McDonagh's dad the day before, and she combed my hair, straight and black like my father's, with a parting on the left and a high quiff rolled back from my forehead.

She reached up to the mantelpiece and took down the small leather purse that had lain there all week beside the clock. MY ROSARY was stamped in gold lettering on the front of the dark-brown purse. Mammy drew the rosary from its leather pouch. She held it out in front of me like a necklace and the crucified Jesus swung hypnotically to-and-fro in the kitchen. 'Hold them up to be blessed after Mass,' Mammy said, 'along with your prayer-book.'

The prayer-book was beautiful. My mother wiped her hands on a towel before she lifted it out from the top shelf of the glass case. Its hard cover gleamed like a white silvery sea-shell; MY FIRST

COMMUNION was emblazoned in gold lettering across the top of its enamelled whiteness. Below that inscription, taking up nearly all the front cover, was a picture of a golden chalice, surrounded by sunrise rays and, above the chalice, a dove-white communion host inscribed with the letters IHS. Everybody knew that these letters stood for what Jesus himself had said: 'I Have Suffered.' When you turned the prayer-book sideways the edges of the pages made a narrow wall of gold that was more precious than anything I had ever held in my hands. The book told the story of the Mass in pictures, from the arrival of the priest onto the altar, through to the priest reading from the Gospel, on to the priest raising the sacred host aloft over his head at the consecration and then, later, placing the communion on the tongue of a boy, like me, who was receiving his First Communion.

'That's you all ready,' my mother said. 'I better make myself presentable now.'

I watched as she did her mouth. She took the gold cap from the tube of lipstick and pushed at the tube until the narrow, angled stick of red stuff stuck out from the shiny cylinder. She took the small square of mirror from the mantelpiece and, making an O of her mouth, painted her wide lips a deep shade of red. The line of red edged outwards at the corners of her mouth, and she wet the tip of her finger with her tongue and wiped away the excess colour. With deft strokes of the big blue comb she teased her dark hair into the waves that I loved, and then she fixed the big, multicoloured scarf around her head, with her hair peeping out at the front and the long peaks of the scarf tied under her chin. With her wine-red coat buttoned up and belted around her narrow waist she was more beautiful than any other boy's mother.

'We'll go out nice and quietly now, so as not to waken the others,' she said. She looked at the clock on the mantelpiece and went on: 'If we leave now, we'll be in good time.'

The clock said twenty-five past eight. Mass in the church in town was at nine o'clock, but we had been told by Brother Edmond to be there at a quarter to nine.

We tiptoed together down the stone hallway to our front door. It was early June but the morning was grey and chilly. The Barracks, too, was blanketed with greyness. The walls and buildings closed in upon us, heavy with the silence of Sunday. In a little while the soldiers would line up to march out through the Gate to the chapel for nine o'clock Mass, but for now the vast square of the parade-ground was silent, deserted.

At the Gate I stayed close to my mother as Bartley drew back the heavy bolt to allow us through, but he appeared to have forgotten the incident of the day of the inspection. He would have begun his duty not long before, at eight o'clock; a long Sunday stretched ahead of him. He seemed preoccupied as he bade us good morning, although he remembered to remind me, as so many others had done, to say a prayer for him when I received my First Communion.

The heavy door of the Gate fell shut behind us. We crossed the tarred road and turned left into the Line. Close by, the lights shone pale in the soldiers' chapel: the first Mass, at eight o'clock, would be coming to an end about now. You couldn't receive your First Communion there, because it was just the soldiers' chapel, so you had to go into town, to St Patrick's. I'd made my first confession there two days earlier, whispering my sins in the gloomy box, later whispering my three Hail Mary's as a penance at the altar-rail. St Patrick's was okay, but it lacked the familiar magic, the friendly statues, the shining linoleum of our own chapel.

The Line was separated from the railway by four strands of smooth wire linking a string of wooden posts. Both Line and railway ran along the top of a high causeway that began at the Barracks and ended at the railway station. When you were used to walking the Line, you marked it off in your mind in sections. The first piece was all downhill, the small chapel on your right, then the stretch of plots where Art's father and some of the other soldiers grew potatoes and onions and cabbages. Sometimes, if you were hungry and the place was deserted, you'd climb through the wires into the plots and pick a handful of the fresh young scallions that grew in the summertime and you'd peel off the outside, clayey skin from the onion-bulb before biting into the crisp, veined flesh inside. This morning my mother and I barely looked at the early potato stalks rising above the brown ridges, their green leaves glistening with the morning dew.

After the downward hill there was a straight stretch until you reached the first bridge on the Line. We called it Paddy Walsh's bridge. Mammy and I blessed ourselves as we crossed the wooden bridge. 'Don't forget to say a prayer for Paddy today after your Communion,' she said to me.

I looked down, as I always did, at the rough cross of stones laid out on the grass below the bridge which spanned a wide gap in the causeway, creating a link between the land on either side of the railway. The stone cross was a memorial to the soldier who had given his name to the bridge when he fell to his death on the grass below. Legend had it that Paddy Walsh, hearing a train approaching in the darkness, and mistakenly thinking that he was walking on the sleepers of the railway, had clambered, as he thought, through the wires to the safety of the Line, but instead had plunged to his death where the stones had now settled deeply into the grass. I wondered how that unknown soldier had felt, when his groping feet had not found the familiar boards of the bridge, but stumbled instead into the freefall darkness. You wouldn't have time to finish saying the Act of Contrition before you hit the ground, but surely it would be guarantee enough of salvation if you managed to whisper the opening words, 'Oh, my God, I am heartily sorry . . .' Surely Jesus would forgive you all your sins if you said as much of the prayer as you could?

The longest section of the Line ran from Paddy Walsh's bridge to the middle bridge. On either side lay the wet, marshy ground which stretched on one side to the salt-water lake, and on the other to the bay.

From the middle bridge Mammy and I moved on briskly until our shoes clumped on Lough Atalia bridge. It was by far the biggest bridge on the Line, spanning the wide neck of water that passed between lake and bay. If you were crossing this bridge at the same time as a train was pulling in or out, you could feel the bridge tremble and groan under the clanking mass of iron, and sometimes the engine would hiss violently and clouds of smoky steam would billow around you.

Once you had crossed Lough Atalia bridge, your journey on the Line was effectively over. The gaping barn-mouth of the station could be seen ahead, journey's end for trains that had travelled across the country all the way from Dublin. The Line veered right, away from the glass cage of the signalman's box, past the low cottage where Ollie McCormack lived, up the hill over the turning-circle where the railwaymen pushed the engine around on the great turning mechanism, so that the engine faced outwards for the next journey . . . From this highest point of the Line you could see down to the grey front of the railway station and, beyond it, the black railings of the Square.

'Nearly there,' Mammy said.

We pushed on down the hill. The road outside the station was empty: no buses ran today. At the corner of the Square we turned right, now only a few minutes walk from the church. On the footpath on the other side of the road a woman waved and called out 'Good morning' and my mother answered her. Beside the woman walked a boy from my class, but he wasn't one of my pals, and I was glad when Mammy made no move to cross the road and walk up to the church with the other woman. It seemed right that we should finish this final stretch of our private journey alone, together.

When the priest placed the small white wafer on my tongue, I could taste nothing. I closed my eyes and my mouth more tightly, but still no hint of taste settled on my tongue. I blessed myself, opened my eyes and stood up from the altar-rail where I had knelt with the other boys. I joined my hands in the position of prayer and took my place in the line of boys going back to their seats. The three benches at the front were reserved for us. Parents and friends sat in the seats behind. Some boys had both parents present. As I walked back I smiled at my mother, sitting on the outside of a seat just a couple of rows back. She smiled back at me.

When you got back to your seat you had to kneel down, bend your face forward into the palms of both hands, and offer prayers of praise and thanks to Jesus. I was praying as hard as I could and trying not to look through the lattice-work of my fingers pressed against my eyes, when I was seized by a mild panic. I was not able to swallow the communion: it was stuck to the roof of my mouth. I pushed my tongue desperately against the edge of the wafer, but it refused to budge. My whole mouth felt dry. When I tried to swallow I made a gulping, harrumphing sound which caused the boy in front of me to turn around and stare at me. I wondered why he was smiling. You were supposed to be serious when you received communion and prayed to Jesus. The fellow beside me was poking his finger into his open mouth. You weren't supposed to do that, because it was a terrible sin for anybody except the priest to touch the body of Jesus. I was pondering the consequences of such poking about when I realised that the communion was no longer in my mouth at all. Whether it had melted, or whether I had unknowingly swallowed it, I couldn't tell. Maybe this was part of the way in which Jesus, mysteriously present in the communion wafer, worked his way into your soul.

After the adults had received Communion and returned to their seats, a shared restlessness seemed to take possession of our three rows at the front. White handkerchiefs, carefully folded and positioned so that precise triangles were visible above breast pockets, were now withdrawn from those pockets and noses were blown with a great variety of noises. Some of the boys wore ties which were suddenly too constricting, so that shirt buttons had to be opened and the unaccustomed neckwear hung lower. Purses were opened and rosary beads swung like catapults. The Brother, his white collar gleaming inside his black suit, hushed us, but his clucking was half-hearted, as if he too wished it were over. It seemed to take hours for the priest to tell us, yet again, that our bodies were now sanctified by the presence of Jesus, and that we must now behave better than we had ever done before. Finally, all the blessings were ended – the new rosary beads all held up, the shining white prayer-books, the brown scapulars and miraculous medals, ourselves last of all.

And we crowded eagerly into the central aisle of the small church. I had to push my way through the crowd to reach my mother, standing just inside the porch at the back of the church. I reached out my hand to her, and she took it in hers, and drew me to her. She said nothing, but held me close against her in the press of people, and then she bent over me and kissed me and my face felt wet but when I looked up she was smiling through the tears that shone in her pale grey-blue eyes. The throng of people ebbed and flowed around us, but we were a separate island in the sea of navy suits and white shirts, and I realised that it mattered not at all that I felt no different now, although I had received my First Communion; what mattered was that this island was always there, no matter what seas swelled around me; what mattered was the scent of my mother's perfume in my nostrils and the certainty that her hand would always reach out to draw me in to safe harbour.

SIX

Two important events took place in the Married Quarters every Friday: the postman brought the cheque and the coalman brought the coal. The two events were not related, but the one had to happen before the other.

The postman had to come first. He wasn't really a postman, just a young soldier who was given the task of taking the letters from the Or'ly Room (as everybody called the Orderly Room) and delivering them to the Married Quarters. The postman did his round every day, but Friday was the day that all the women of the Quarters looked forward to. Friday was when the postman brought the cheque. The men got their wages once a week from the officers and the mothers got their cheques once a week from the postman. If there were five kids in the family, as in ours, then your mother got a bigger cheque than Paul O'Dowd's mother, because Paul had no brothers or sisters. And your mother's cheque was bigger if your dad was a sergeant, like mine, than Bobby's mother's cheque, because *his* dad was only a three-star. These details of the workings of the military financial machine were familiar to all of the pals and myself; picked up as effortlessly as learning to drass a bicycle wheel or whistle a tune. The other thing you learned about the cheque was that it was never enough.

After the cheque came on Friday morning Mammy put on her coat and gathered up her two shopping-bags to go to town where she would cash the cheque in the Munster and Leinster Bank and buy the messages for the week. The cheque was always examined first, simply to make sure it was not less than the ordained amount, before being folded and placed in the handbag which in turn was stowed in the good red shopping-bag. You'd see your mother doing all these things on the Fridays of the school-holidays. When school was open you'd see none of it, but you'd be looking forward to getting home from school on Friday because you'd know it was cheque-day and Mammy would have the *Beano* waiting for you on the table in the kitchen after her trip to town.

It was no mere case of consternation when the cheque failed to arrive, as sometimes happened. Non-arrival of the manila envelope, officially franked and bearing the oval-printed legend *An Roinn Cosanta*, was a catastrophe for the entire household.

Your mother watched the postman, looking through the net-curtained window, while he walked around the corner of the Quarters to Number 1. Mammy had her hair combed and her coat and scarf on; the two shopping-bags hung by their straps from the arm of the oak armchair beside the range. In a moment, you knew, the postman would pass by the window again and you'd run to the front door, anticipating his knock, and say thank you, and you'd run back along the stone-floored hallway, bearing the cheque like a prize to your waiting mother.

Sometimes it didn't happen that way. You'd open the outside door and the postman wouldn't be standing on the doorstep. He'd be halfway already to the door of Number 3, but he'd sense you looking after him, and he'd turn and look at you from under his peaked cap, and he'd shrug and say apologetically: 'Yours must've got delayed today – it'll probably be in the next post.'

The next post was hours away, and it was useless. You couldn't make it in time along the Line to town before the bank closed at three o'clock. Sometimes the manager in the soldiers' canteen would cash the cheque for you as a favour, but everybody knew that the canteen closed at half past one and didn't open again until half five. You could try taking the cheque to the little shop at the far end of the military road, but that could be tricky if you'd already run up a fair bit on the slate with the shopkeeper, because he might expect you to pay off more from your bill than you could afford to hand over out of a single cheque.

You didn't run back up the stone hallway to tell your mother that the cheque might come in the next post. Your feet dragged on the stone floor. You pushed the door open into the kitchen reluctantly. Your mother knew. She always knew, and you could never figure out how she always knew. She didn't turn around to face you. She stared out the window although you sensed that she didn't even see the armourer's shop opposite Number 2. She opened the box of Woodbines and drew out a cigarette. The match flared and sizzled in the quiet kitchen and you wished you had any other kind of news to tell her.

'He didn't have it,' Mammy would say, drawing noisily on the cigarette.

'He said it'll probably come in the next post,' you'd tell her.

Sometimes Mammy seemed far away, as if she were not really there in Number 2. She'd puff on her cigarette, and go on looking through the window, and she'd be silent for a while, as if she were gone to visit somewhere in her head. In a way I understood this: there were occasions at the teatime table when I found it necessary to remove myself from the childish squabbles of my younger brothers and sisters and take off with Kit Carson on horseback across the wide-open plains of Wyoming. Maybe Mammy had her own Wyoming to visit while she stood there at the kitchen window, left arm folded across her chest, cigarette poised and smoking between the fingers of her upraised right hand.

She'd be herself again when she'd come back from visiting her personal Wyoming. You could see her sort of shake herself, like a puppy coming out of the sea, and then she'd cross the kitchen briskly and she'd lift the kettle with one hand from the top of the range and she'd drop the cigarette butt, red now from the lipstick applied in expectation of her trip to town, into the fire, and she'd put the kettle down firmly again on the range and she'd say: 'Sure what of it? It'll come when it comes, and we'll be all right anyway.'

You knew it was all right then, but you also knew it *wasn't* all right.

It was all right again because Mammy said so.

But you knew about the things that she didn't mention.

The insurance man calling that afternoon for his two-shillings-a-week.

The *Beano* that you couldn't get in Holland's shop beside the bus-stop.

The coal-truck pulling up in the space outside the armourer's shop and the driver and his helper doing the rounds of the Quarters, their blackened faces still cheerful as they shouldered the hundredweight bags with seemingly effortless ease. There was no coal if the cheque didn't come. You could ask for the bag and promise to pay the following week, but the driver always said no. 'The boss'd kill me, Missus,' he'd say, and you'd know he hated having to refuse you. 'Sure he has every one of them oul' bags counted himself, and I have to account for the lot of them.'

The coal didn't matter in the summertime. Most weeks in the summer Mammy didn't buy coal at all, but some summer Fridays she liked to buy a bag, just to have as a safeguard against a bad week in winter. 'It's no harm to think ahead when you have a little to spare,' Mammy would say. Then she'd laugh at herself: 'Listen to me – sure we don't even have enough for the day that's in it, let alone have something to spare.'

If the non-arrival of the cheque on Friday was a catastrophe, then the arrival of the 'big cheque' was, at best, a major inconvenience. The term 'big cheque' did not, in this instance, refer to the amount of money which the cheque was worth; rather it referred to the physical dimensions of the cheque. You knew when Mammy opened the manila envelope and groaned as she withdrew the contents that yet again a 'big cheque' had arrived.

'Well, bad cess to them and their big cheques,' she'd exclaim. 'Do they think I have nothing better to be doin' than to be going around gettin' cheques signed?'

When my mother said 'bad cess' to somebody, you knew it was serious. Who 'they' were – those nameless, faceless senders of 'big cheques' – was unclear; what was clear to me was that 'they' were causing Mammy severe inconvenience, and deserved chastisement, like any pesky critters, from the hands of Kit Carson or Buck Jones . . .

Everybody knew that you couldn't just bring the 'big cheque' into the bank to get it cashed. Everybody knew that first you had to get the cheque signed by the chaplain or, if you couldn't locate him, by the superintendent of the Gardaí or even by the bank manager himself. The chaplain always did it, if he was around, but sometimes he'd be 'away', my father would explain to Mammy, and she'd bristle at the thought of having to ask the garda superintendent for his signature or, worse still, the bank manager.

'The last time I had to get the bank manager to sign it, I was mortified,' Mammy told us. 'Asking me all sorts of questions, about how many children I have and what rank is your father. I had a good mind to tell him that I was cashing my cheque in his bank for

years past and that if he was doin' his business right he wouldn't
have to be askin' me all these questions because he'd know me
himself.'

'And did you tell him that, Mammy?' I asked.

My mother laughed. 'God help your head,' she said to me, 'if
you think that the likes of us could be saying something like that to
the bank manager.'

'Why couldn't we?' I wanted to know. My mother had the right
to ask anybody anything, or say whatever she felt like.

She measured me with a look. 'That's the why.'

'But – '

'No "buts", Kevin, that's the why.'

I filed the problem away in my mind, yet another topic to be
broached again at a more favourable moment. I could ask Mammy
anything, but I had learned that some topics demanded careful
choice of timing, especially topics that were peremptorily shut off
with 'that's the why'.

I could bide my time. Life in the Barracks was rich and full of
intriguing people and places. I had good pals, trusted companions
who could be relied upon to face any foe, confront any challenge.
There were mountains to climb, burning deserts to cross. Best of
all, there was Mammy and her talk: you'd start off having a chat
about that stupid big cheque and you'd end up with the conundrum
of why you couldn't say certain things to the bank manager.

Although it wasn't really much of a puzzle, I asked Art for his
opinion later that evening, as we rested our mounts on the crest of
an especially steep stretch of the Oregon Trail. Art scanned the
horizon with shaded eyes before answering. We'd passed a burnt-
out cabin earlier that day and knew there were renegade Redskins
on the warpath.

'I suppose,' said Art, shifting in the saddle to look at me, 'I
suppose that a bank manager is an officer.'

I knew he was right: in my own heart I had known it all along.

It was freezing cold and the cheque hadn't arrived. Mammy had
saved the last of the coal for frying the piece of round steak for my
father's tea and for boiling the big silver kettle with the swan neck.
The kitchen was cold when we sat at the table that evening. The
curtains were closed across the two high windows, but you could

almost sense the cold outside from the sharp clarity of boots ringing on the stone outside as people hurried home.

There was an unaccustomed quietness about the table; even Jacky was silent. My father was rapt in the racing results from Haydock. It was Danny who broke the silence.

'I'm cold, Mammy,' he said. He was only learning to talk; sometimes you had to laugh at his baby-speech.

His words made my father look up from the folded newspaper. 'The fire's going out,' he said, looking at my mother.

'There's no coal,' Mammy said. She didn't look at him as she spoke.

I watched my father shift himself in the armchair at the other end of the table. I watched the lines crease his forehead and the question form on his lips. 'No coal? Why?'

'It ran out,' my mother said. 'It was a cold week.' She went on jigging my sister, Martha, on her lap in the easy motion that would eventually lull the baby into sleep.

'But it'll be days yet before the coalman comes again,' my father said, 'it's only Wednesday – '

'We had to use more coal this week,' Mammy cut in, 'and there was nothing I could do.'

'But – '

'There's no "buts",' Mammy interrupted again. 'D'you think I have spare money to be putting aside for extra coal when the weather turns as cold as this?' She stood up from the table, holding the baby on her hip.

'You should have asked me,' my father said.

We watched and listened to this exchange between our parents in silence. No bread was buttered, no arm reached across the table for the pot of jam. For a moment Mammy looked at my father before turning sharply and leaving the kitchen.

'I'm cold,' Danny said again, but Miriam hushed him before he could do any more babbling. I avoided my father's glance. I made sure I didn't catch Jacky's eye either: you never knew what he might come out with. The silence weighed upon the kitchen while Mammy was out of the room. We heard her step crossing the stone hallway, lighter now, and we knew that Martha had been put into her cot.

When Mammy came back into the kitchen she didn't close the door behind her. I looked across at her, standing in the doorway with her hand on the brass knob, and she smiled sadly at me. 'I'm after lighting a fire in the grate in the bedroom,' she said. 'Let ye hurry up with your lessons and then ye can go across to the fire.'

'A fire in the bedroom!' Jacky shouted with glee. 'A fire in the bedroom!' We were silent while Jacky pushed his chair noisily back from the table. Mammy's hand touched his head of dark hair as he dashed past her.

'And be quiet over there!' Mammy said to him. 'Martha's asleep in the back room.'

Doors opened and banged shut loudly in the wake of Jacky's departure but, though we listened, there came no sound of baby-crying. The kitchen fell quiet again.

'Why did you light a fire in the bedroom, Mammy?' Miriam's question was the one I wanted to ask myself, but was too cautious to ask in the strained silence.

'I only got a few blocks, *a ghrá*,' Mammy answered, 'and they're too big to fit into the range.' She moved across the kitchen until she stood beside Miriam's chair. 'They're more like small logs than blocks,' Mammy said, smiling. 'I have a couple of them in the grate now, and they're that big they're hanging out of it.'

'The house might go on fire, Mammy!'

'Indeed it won't, pet,' my mother said to her, laughing, 'not unless your brother Jacky gets up to his tricks over there – why don't you go on across to the bedroom now and keep an eye on him for me?' Miriam hesitated, looking at the cups and plates on the table. 'Don't mind the washing-up at all,' Mammy said, 'Sure Kevin will give me a hand, won't you?'

I nodded. In my mind I could see Jacky hauling burning logs from the fireplace and turning the entire Barracks into a conflagra-tion. 'You go on,' I said to Miriam. 'I'll do it.'

'Have you the lessons done?' Mammy asked her.

'I only had tables to learn – two and two are four!' Miriam's voice rose in scorn. 'Sure they're simple!'

'Off with you so, pet.'

At the kitchen door Miriam paused and turned back. 'Mammy?'

'What is it?'

'Can I sit up on your bed beside the fire?'

My mother laughed. 'Sure you can of course.'

'I won't toss it,' Miriam said.

'I know you won't; now hurry across before your brother has the place wrecked.'

Miriam's pigtails swung as she hurried from the room. The kitchen felt empty, silent.

'Where did you get the blocks?' my father asked in a quiet voice.

'John Lovett left me in a bag this morning,' Mammy said.

John Lovett was a CS, a company-sergeant. He was unmarried, and lived in a room across from the Married Quarters. All the boys in the Quarters liked him.

'I don't like us to be taking charity,' my father said.

'It wasn't charity,' Mammy said. 'He just brought me a bag of blocks when the men were drawing coal for the Officers' Mess.' Every day of the week the big gates of the coalyard were open for the private soldiers to draw fuel for the billets and the messes. The gates were closed and padlocked each evening around four o'clock.

'I just don't like it,' my father repeated.

'What am I supposed to do?' Mammy asked. 'Let the children go cold?'

'I'll see what I can do in the morning,' my father said at length. 'I'll try to organise something from the coalyard.'

I noticed how my mother's face warmed into a smile at my father's words, but I was only half-listening to this exchange between them. I was trying to imagine a bedroom with a fire in it, the logs crackling in the grate, shadows dancing on the curtains and you could sit on the soft bed and feel the heat warming your insides . . . just like cowboys around the campfire after a busy day branding steers . . .

I felt my mother's hand on my shoulder. 'Are you back with us again?' she laughed at me. 'C'mon, give me a hand with the dishes and then you can get at your lessons.' She smiled at me and the kitchen was warm again.

Mammy must have saved a few lumps of coal, for there was a red glow behind the bars of the range the next morning. The fire spluttered and crackled from the small pieces of kindling she'd mixed with the coal. The kettle steamed on the hot-spot above the fire; beside it, the saucepan of porridge bubbled hoarsely. The teapot sat on the hob, warming itself while it waited for its fill of tea-leaves and boiling water.

We ate our porridge quietly. Something of the gravity of the situation had conveyed itself to us the night before. It had been no companionable campfire that we had sat around in my parents' bedroom the previous night; rather it had been a half-hearted pile of damp wood that fizzled and spluttered and blazed intermittently and reluctantly. The novelty of sitting on the big army bed had died, literally, like a damp squib. Our goodnights had been subdued as we'd slunk, unusually early, to the warmth of our own beds.

Porridge was stuff that I generally only tolerated, but this morning I was glad to tuck into the thick, warming mess. We'd opened the curtains and, though it was still dark outside, you could tell that it was a raw morning. Through the small panes of glass you could see the grey clouds scudding across the Barracks wall before the November wind.

'Will I come home at lunch-hour, Mammy?' I asked.

She was standing bent over the range, the kettle in her hand, pouring the boiling water into the shining metal teapot. 'Why wouldn't you come home? Don't you always come home for your dinner?' The Barracks fellows raced from the Brothers' school up Shop Street to catch the bus at ten to one, wolfed down their dinners in a few minutes and then walked, ran or sauntered back along the Line as the mood took us. The entire round trip took no more than fifty minutes. 'Why wouldn't you come home for your dinner?' she asked again.

'I just thought – ' I fidgeted, unable to say aloud what was worrying me.

I needn't have worried: my mother knew. 'Don't mind about the fire,' she said, 'I'll find something to boil the spuds.'

My father went on shining the yellow buttons on his tunic. He'd moved his armchair back from the table to stand beside the glass case. The tin of Brasso stood on the front ledge of the glass case, the narrow neck of the tin crammed with the milky substance that first dulled and then burnished the buttons. My father stood with his left foot up on the chair, his green bull's-wool tunic draped across his left knee. He worked, as usual, with avid concentration and easy rhythm. The button-stick was the essential tool of the operation – a piece of thin, shining brass about six or seven inches long and a couple of inches wide, with a narrow slit cut along the centre of the stick for about three-quarters of its length. You half-

Standing to attention with Corporal Joe Burke, a friend of my father, at the doorway to Number 20, our first home in the Married Quarters; you can see the shadow of the veranda railings on the grey stone walls.

'The square itself was a two-tier tablecloth of white: there was no hint in the
still air of the excited shouts and yelps that had been flung from the
chairoplanes and swinging boats last summer, when Mammy had taken me
in one evening to Tofts.'

May Fair Galway.

'The dark road was slick with rain-washed cow dung after the cattle fair of the morning. The wet dung shone under the yellow light that spilled down from the glass doors of the railway hotel.'

'She shivered a moment, her slight body trembling in the chill, and her gaze swept round, as if she were seeing anew the stone chapel and the grey Barracks and the lighted Gate, and, behind me, the Line threading its way above the Furze towards the town.'

Taoiseach Eamon de Valera was conferred with the Freedom of Galway in 1950. Dev inspected this guard of honour, made up of soldiers from our Barracks, to mark the occasion. Counting from right to left, my father is the eleventh soldier in the guard of honour.

An early picture of Mammy in her own backyard, accompanied by Uncle Tim's greyhound, Mutt, reputedly the winner of some local races.

'You couldn't see the school from the road … There were tall windows glinting in the white glare, taller than any I had seen in the Barracks, and the doorway in the corner of the quadrangle was bigger and wider than the entrance of the Gate.'

'Unseen, hidden by the walls of the Barracks, but clearly etched in the mind's eye, the sergeant and officer of the guard stood to attention beside the white flagpole while the lowering of the flag marked the end of another military day.'

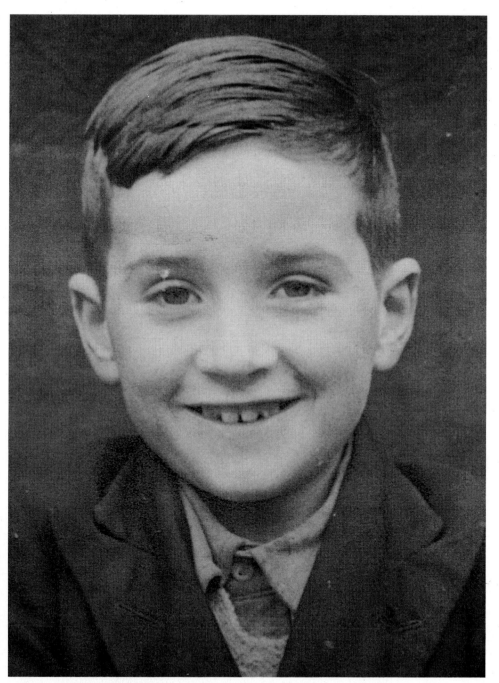

' "What's the 'T' for?" Brother Matthew asked, smiling.
"It's for Thomas, my middle name," I told him, seriously. The Brother seemed
to be trying to hold laughter in, although I could see nothing to laugh at ...'

'With deft strokes of the big blue comb, she teased her dark hair into the waves that I loved, and then she fixed the big multicoloured scarf around her head, with her hair peeping out at the front and the long peaks of the scarf tied under her chin.'

crumpled, half-folded the fabric of the tunic so that three or four of the buttons nestled in this centre slit like yellow, curved heads. You took the soft yellow chamois cloth in your right hand and, with the same hand, picked up the tin of Brasso and upended it against the cloth. You shook the tin vigorously; you could hear the metallic liquid slurping inside. When you put the tin down there was a small dark stain on the yellow cloth. This you applied to the tunic buttons; the tunic itself was protected against the Brasso by the breadth of the button-stick. The Brasso made the golden buttons dull and dark. You worked your way through the big buttons down the centre and the smaller ones that fastened the pockets of the tunic, until they had all been dulled with their coat of Brasso. Then you took the soft cloth, the polishing one, and you worked the magic on all the buttons until they gleamed like Spanish treasure and even the spaces between the tiny strings of the harps embossed on all the buttons were miniature ribbons of gold. You had to shine your cap-badge and your collar-badges in the same way. The button-stick itself shone like a thin wafer of gold from the continual polishing. I'd tried to describe the operation once to one of the civvies at school, but I'd given up in frustration, unable to find words to describe even the button-stick. It was simpler to stick with Art and the other lads in the Barracks: at least they knew what you were talking about.

When Miriam and I left to catch the bus to school that morning, my father was buckling the brown belt of his tunic. The leather of the belt was soft and supple from years of polishing. His red-brown boots and short, ankle-high leggings gleamed. My mother called out to us, as always, to bless ourselves. Dipping my finger in the holy-water font beside the door, I could not help glancing at the coal-tub in the scullery. The blackened wrought-iron tub was, as I could have told without looking, quite empty.

My eyes were watering in the cutting wind that blew in from the bay. Bobby cupped his hands together and blew into them noisily. He did a little dance on the pile of coal-waste, and the burnt-out fragments crunched under the metal studs of his black boots. 'I'm free-eezing!' he hooted into his cupped hands. 'I don't think I'm ever going to be warm again!' His muffled words floated away on the icy wind over Paddy Walsh's bridge. In the near-distance the green, white and gold flag was stretched taut from the flagpole above the Barracks. Beyond the whin-covered marshland that we called 'the Furze', the dark sea crashed unceasingly on the stony shore.

'We better get a move on,' I shouted to Bobby.

He grinned back at me. Like myself, he wore a bottle-green balaclava that exposed only his eyes, nose and mouth. The balaclava was a badge of a Barracks-lad: if ever you saw a boy from the town wearing one, you looked at him a second time, as if he were trespassing or trying to pass himself off as something he was not.

We picked up our half-full sandbags and slithered halfway down the slope from the railway line. We moved, however, with practised caution: we both wore short corduroy trousers and knee-length socks, and the jagged fragments of coal could cut painfully through the woollen socks. The railway embankment was covered with coal waste. We'd already picked the best of it on top of the bank, poking with our hands and boots among the dust and useless husks, searching for the smooth unburnt pieces that would light the range at home. Most of the waste from the trains was useless: pockmarked shards, like misshapen apple-butts, that had their fire already burned out of them in the steam engines.

Only a single line of railway track ran from our town out under the Barracks bridge and on through the unknown towns that marked the route to Dublin. There was a shunting-line, however, that stretched from the station to a pair of buffers set in a concrete platform at Paddy Walsh's bridge. To this spot came the wagons bearing the waste and used coal from the steam-powered engines that hauled the lines of carriages along the shining track. We'd often watched the railway workmen unhinge the sides of the wagons and shovel the black waste out onto the sloping bank. Earlier that day, watching the pitiful fire that failed to warm the kitchen of Number 2 at lunch-hour, the idea had come to me. Once or twice I'd seen civvies picking among the black waste near Paddy Walsh's bridge: why couldn't I do it myself?

Bobby alone had agreed to come coal-picking with me after school. I hadn't asked Paul O'Dowd; even if his mother had consented, Paul himself would never commit his soft plumpness to the filth, dust and jagged fragments. Art and Tommy had demurred, and I couldn't blame them: the cold numbed my fingers and the soft flesh above my knees was scalded red from the combination of cutting wind and rough corduroy. I could feel the particles of coal dust tickling the inside of my nose and I sneezed. Bobby laughed. 'Your nose is all black from the coal,' he said.

'So is yours.' It wasn't just his nose. There were daubs of coal-black under his eyes and on his upper lip. We both laughed inanely. For the moment the cutting wind was forgotten along with the empty coal-tub in the scullery.

Suddenly Bobby jerked into stillness. He laid his right index finger against his lips in a gesture for silence and inclined his head in a listening attitude. 'D'you hear it?' he asked me. It was the bugler playing his last notes of the working day in the Barracks. Whatever way the wind had turned, it was carrying the bugle notes to us from inside the grey walls on the hill.

We looked towards the Barracks. Dimly, in the fading light, we could just make out the slowly descending tricolour, as it was lowered gently along the flagpole on top of the Magazine. Unseen, hidden by the walls of the Barracks, but clearly etched in the mind's eye, the sergeant and the officer of the guard stood to attention beside the white flagpole while the lowering of the flag marked the end of another military day. And below them, on the edge of the Square where the soldiers paraded every morning, stood the bugler, erect in the dusky light, his fingers tapping the shining stops, his lips blowing the haunting notes across the dying day.

That end-of-day refrain never failed to move me. It stirred something deep inside me, the memory of a loneliness that I had never known personally, echoes from streets I had never walked in, towns I had never visited, beyond even the very ends of the shining railway tracks I now stood beside. The bugle-notes lingered and died under the leaden skies.

'Let's go home,' I said to Bobby, 'sure the bags are nearly full anyway.'

We hauled the bags up the bank. At the top we tamped them firmly against a wooden sleeper to let our scavenged coal settle into the sandbags. A cloud of black dust blew up into our faces and we both burst out laughing again.

'Bend down,' Bobby said. I bent towards him, for he was a good deal shorter than I, and he wet his finger and then I felt his damp finger tracing lines across my cheeks. 'Black for warpaint,' he chanted in his deepest voice.

'Death to the white man,' I growled. I wet my own finger with spittle and daubed a cross on either side of Bobby's nose.

'We take-um white man's scalp at the Gate,' Bobby intoned.

'Um White man at the Gate heap scared of Apache warriors!' I shouted. We roared with laughter. It was funnier because we knew that Big Bartley was on duty at the Gate. 'We tell-um Bartley that um bags are full of scalps and fire-water for Apache braves!'

We hoisted the bags on our shoulders and began to run along the Line towards the Barracks. Our steps were measured by the railway sleepers. The bags bounced on our backs. We whooped Apache-style as we went.

As we crossed Paddy Walsh's bridge, we remembered to bless ourselves.

The street area in front of the Married Quarters was full of children playing as Bobby and I made our way down the steps from the tarred area outside the armourer's shop. The area we played on was not so smooth: potholes yawned like craters in the rough gravelled surface, and between every two homes ran a shallow drain which carried the surface water from the veranda above. Wounded knees and shins were a recurring feature of the Barracks landscape. The area itself was well sheltered from the knifing wind. The perimeter walls of the Barracks bounded the two narrow ends of the strip of ground, and the two long sides of the rectangle were protected from the wind by the bulk of the Married Quarters block and, opposite, the various buildings housed in the interior of the Barracks terrain.

Bobby and I stopped outside Number 2. The green door was open on the unlighted hallway. Miriam, in the act of closing the curtains on the kitchen windows, tapped on the window when she spotted us outside. We stood waving back to her until the curtains closed on her smiling face and long pigtails.

Together Bobby and I studied our two bags of coal. What had seemed such extravagant booty on the freezing railway bank looked almost pathetic now – two small sandbags leaning against each other outside the door of Number 2. I said as much to Bobby.

'Your Mammy won't think so,' he said, grinning, 'if you have no coal at all in the house.'

I looked keenly at his coal-stained face looking out from the balaclava. Bobby was the same age as the rest of us, yet his words sometimes seemed laden with a wisdom beyond his years. 'Do you think so?' I asked him uncertainly. The bag of coal looked as if it would be lost in a corner of the empty coal-tub.

'Wait 'n' see,' Bobby said, 'wait 'n' see.'

I gave him a hand up with the bag on his shoulder, reflecting on yet another mystery of existence: that a boy like Bobby could utter such wisdom while so many adults, who always insisted that they knew best, could come out with such codswallop.

'One for all,' I said to Bobby.

'And all for one,' he replied. I watched him for a moment, threading his way among the knots of boys and girls who were involved in various games under the Barracks lights. 'Make way for the coalman!' he called out. 'Make way for the coalman!'

Some of the smaller kids took up the cry. 'Bob-by-is-a-coalman!' they chanted. 'Bob-by-is-a-coalman!' They followed him like noisy acolytes as he made his way towards Number 5, the house in The Arch.

I picked up my own bag and stepped into our hallway. The brass knob on the door into our scullery gleamed faintly in the half-dark. The light was off when I pushed the door open and I did not switch it on. I closed the door behind me and shuffled in the darkness of the scullery towards the coal-tub.

The kitchen door swung open and my mother stood there in the rectangle of light from the kitchen. 'Is that you, Kevin?' she asked. 'What're you doing in the dark at all like that?'

I couldn't see her face, with the light behind her, but I could hear the smile and the welcome in her voice. 'It's a surprise, Mammy,' I said, and I couldn't keep the delight out of my voice.

'A surprise, *a ghrá*?' she came closer to me, her arms folded in familiar posture across her thin chest. 'What kind of a surprise?' She reached out her hand to switch on the scullery light and I blinked and grinned triumphantly at her. 'Look at the state of you!' she gasped. 'Sure you're black from head to toe like the coalman himself!'

'I know,' I said happily. 'That's the surprise!' I hadn't told Mammy where I was going when I'd hurried off with Bobby after school, the folded-up sandbag concealed inside my lumberjacket. I watched her eyes travel to the bag of coal, standing open-necked beside me on the stone floor of the scullery, and I prepared myself to receive and revel in the warmth of her praise. I'd earned it, poking with freezing hands in the jagged waste on the railway bank.

My mother stooped over me and I allowed her to peel the balaclava from my head. My ears, released from their woollen cocoon, tingled deliciously; my mother's hands, clasping my face between them, were palms of well-earned grace. 'You're a great boy,' she said, 'but there was no need for you to go pickin' coal on the railway tracks.'

'It was fierce cold down there,' I said to her, my chest swelling with the joy of remembered hardship. I knew now how Kit and the settlers had felt after the wagon-train had battled its way over snow-bound mountains to the rich, wide-open grasslands of the West. 'Bobby and myself were *frozen* out there,' I added for emphasis.

'You're a great boy,' she said again. 'Now let's clean all this coal-dirt off you.'

Was that it? I wondered. A modicum of faint praise for endurance above and beyond the call of duty? I heard the concern in her voice, and it was for more than the black on my face.

I saw the coaltub from the corner of my eye.

I saw the black lumps gleaming in it.

I turned, escaping from my mother's arms, and looked, bewildered, at the cast-iron tub.

It was heaped high with coal.

My mother's gaze met mine and she reached out to touch me but I drew back from her. 'Your Daddy managed to get some from the coalyard,' she said gently.

I brushed away the hot tears edging from my eyes. I began to sob and this time I made no resistance when she knelt beside me and put her arms around me.

'It doesn't matter, *a ghrá* – I'm still very proud of you for doing it.' She held me away from her at arm's length then, and said: 'Anyway, aren't you pleased that your Daddy went and got the coal for us?'

I didn't answer. I leaned my head upon my mother's shoulder and in my gulped tears I felt the bitter-sad taste of ambition thwarted. She held me close for a long, long time, until Miriam came out of the kitchen and found us there in the stone scullery. My sister's fingers touched my shoulder quizzically, and I tried to smile at her, but her anxious face swam in the film of my tears and I half-sensed, half-saw the door ajar on the world of grown-ups, where love must be shared and pain is not banished by a healing kiss.

SEVEN

Apart from the civilian tradesmen and labourers who did the maintenance work on the Married Quarters, and the other military buildings, there were a few civvies who came regularly to the Barracks. Most, like the coalman and his helper, came out from the town: every Friday you'd see the insurance man and Joe from Sloan's slowly doing the rounds of the Quarters, collecting their weekly payments – a shilling here, two bob there, sometimes half a crown in the aftermath of Christmas, Holy Communion or Confirmation. Sometimes, if the cheque was late, you had to go to the front door and tell Joe or the insurance man that your Mammy wasn't in, and he'd ask if she had left the money for him, and you'd say no while you looked down at the doorstep and shifted uneasily from foot to foot, and he'd hum-and-haw a bit before moving on to the next house and you'd shut the door relieved that he was gone but hot with a kind of shame for the way he'd looked at you, as if he knew that you were telling fibs, as if he knew all along that your mother was standing behind the inside door in the scullery, smoking a Woodbine. They were, without exception, polite and attentive, those civvie collectors from the town, but there was a whiff of power about their suits and collars-and-ties and their leather-bound record-books that made you feel even smaller, standing on your own scrubbed doorstep. Their civilian presence was an intrusion upon the patterned regularity of our military life.

Not all the civvies who were allowed through the Barracks gates brought with them such intimations of authority. Maura came into the Barracks a couple of times a week to collect the swill from the Married Quarters. She was a small, thin woman with lively eyes in a pretty face. I thought she looked nice, standing on our doorstep, while Mammy ladled into the tin buckets the mess of potato skins and vegetable peelings that we saved for her. Her dark eyes danced and her cheeks glowed like shiny red apples. Not even the smell of the swill from her buckets could taint her aura of vitality. I was always pleased whenever she accepted Mammy's invitation to come in for a cup of tea in her hand.

'I'll have to be quick about it,' she'd say, 'himself will be home soon expectin' his tea.'

'Himself' was a tall, taciturn man that we often met on his bicycle on the Line. I knew from listening to Maura that he worked in the post office. She'd come in then, leaving the lidded buckets of swill in the hall, and sit in front of the range while she had a cup of tea in her hand, and she'd talk about the chickens she kept around her house that seemed to be on the very water's edge. We walked out there sometimes, the other boys and myself, to the small horseshoe bay about half a mile along the railway tracks from the Barracks, and sometimes we'd muse out loud about what it must be like to live so close to the sea. It would be great, we decided wisely, to live there in the summer, but not so hot in the winter. Sometimes, watching her on the armchair in our kitchen, I'd imagine her pushing her own front door shut against the sea and the wind that raged without. But you'd think there was no hardship at all in her life, the way she chatted to Mammy and laughed beside the fire.

'All the same,' Mammy said to her one evening, 'it's a pity you can't get the swill from the Officers' Mess or the cookhouse – sure you'd be away with it then, haven't they loads of it!' The swill from the Barracks dining-rooms was stored in huge barrels that were emptied regularly by a civvie with a horse and cart. He didn't like to let the boys from the Quarters have a spin on his cart.

Maura laughed happily at my mother's words. 'Haven't I enough to do as I am,' she asked, 'bringing my cans in and out the Line with me?' She was a familiar sight on the Line, raincoat buttoned, hurrying along with a tin can in either hand.

'Sure I know you are,' Mammy said, 'but it'd be great for you all the same.'

'You wouldn't be able to go out the Line if you had a horse and cart,' Jacky cut in. 'The cart'd get stuck on the tracks and the train'd crash into it and kill the horse.' He clapped his hands together loudly. Maura laughed, and my mother smiled. I concentrated on my Buck Jones comic, trying to ignore the infantile interruption.

Putting up with younger brothers was a task that did not grow easier.

'Did you hear about the family that broke into the old School-house last night? Maura asked. My ears pricked up at this, but I remained bent over the exploits of Buck Jones on the kitchen table.

'What family? Where?' I could hear the interest inflected in Mammy's voice. Jacky clapped his hands together again to signify, presumably, yet another horse and train crash, but Mammy shushed him angrily. 'Will you have manners and be quiet,' she said. 'Can't you see that Maura is telling me something!' I watched Jacky open his arms wide and swing them frantically towards each other: all of us in the kitchen braced ourselves for the clapping of his palms, but at the last minute his hands froze, inches apart, and he grinned at Mammy. 'You're an oul' cod,' she laughed at him, and I had to smile into my comic. Sometimes you just had to laugh at our Jacky. 'Now – ' Mammy turned again to Maura and there was an edge of excitement in her voice. 'Who broke into the old School?'

Maura drew her chair closer to my mother's and their heads inclined together. The firelight from the range played upon them both – my mother's thick black hair and Maura's steely grey, although she was only about the same age as Mammy. Some of the lads called her 'the silver fox', but only behind her back. I had to strain to hear what she was telling Mammy. 'I thought you knew, because he's a soldier.'

Mammy shook her head: without looking up from my comic I could sense her hurrying Maura along with the information.

'Tynan is his name,' Maura said. 'He's a private here in the Barracks. The first I knew of it was when he knocked on my door early this morning – there was only myself up, the rest of them were still in bed. I got the fright of my life when I opened the door and saw him standing there with a kettle in his hand, asking for water. "Where have you come from?" I asked him. "The old School, ma'am," he says to me. "We broke into it last night, myself and the wife and kids."'

This was more interesting than Buck Jones. We all knew the old Schoolhouse – a grey stone building with high windows standing beside Maura's house. We all thought it a bit of a joke to call it a school, so small and remote it seemed in comparison with the Brothers' school in town.

'He's a fine, tall man with a hard jaw on him,' Maura said, 'but he didn't seem dangerous or anything so I asked him to come into the kitchen. I left him there while I went out to the yard to fill the kettle and when I came back in he thanked me for it. "How did you break in?" I says to him. "It wasn't too hard to get a window open," he says to me. He must have thought I was worried then, because he says to me: "You needn't be afraid or anything, ma'am, we're not thieves or robbers, I just had to get a roof over their heads. We were goin' to be thrown out of the place we were in, and we hadn't a penny, and I knew about the old School bein' empty – I'm a soldier in the Barracks, ma'am – and sure I thought what harm would it do to anybody, sure they have to have a roof over their heads, Ma'am."'

I remained immersed in Buck Jones's Wild West adventures while Maura paused to draw breath and drink her tea. Her drinking was neat and dainty, like all her movements: she perched straight-backed on the edge of her seat with her wellington-clad legs angled back under the chair, crossed at the ankles.

'And the children,' my mother prompted her. 'Tell us about the kids, God help them.'

'They have three children,' Maura said, 'two girls and a boy in the middle.'

'You saw them then!'

'She came around after a while to thank me – I gave himself a can of milk and a grain of tea and sugar and some bread – sure God help us, I couldn't bear to think of the little children in that oul' place, freezing cold and the damp runnin' down the walls . . .'

'What's she like?' Mammy asked.

'A fine, tall woman, God bless her, and good-lookin' too – you'd turn your head to look at her if she passed you on the street.' She finished her tea: the cup jangled on the saucer. Most callers who received 'a cup of tea in your hand' were given a mug, but Mammy always gave Maura a rose-patterned cup and saucer.

'You'll have another drop?'

'I haven't time, thanks,' Maura answered, standing up. She smoothed the skirt of her raincoat and crossed the kichen to place the cup and saucer on the table. 'You're a fierce man for the reading,' she said to me.

'When will you have the next *Far East*?' I asked her.

'Next week,' she said. Maura distributed the *Far East* magazine to about a dozen homes in the Quarters. 'Is it Pudsy you like in it?' she asked me.

'He's great gas all right,' I said. Pudsy Ryan's Diary was a regular feature in the magazine, full of Pudsy's daft accounts of encounters with Sister Alo Wishes and his baby sister, Noreen, all described in Pudsy's own notorious brand of spelling. 'The Brother at school'd kill him for his spelling, though.'

Maura smiled. Her white teeth were small and neat. 'That reminds me,' she said to my mother. 'I'm going to be looking for the two bob for the *Far East* next month as well.'

'There's always something to be paid,' Mammy said, but there was no hint of real complaint in her voice. 'Anyway, sure we could be worse off, like that poor family out in the Schoolhouse.'

'Bare walls and bare floors,' Maura said.

'Have they no few sticks of furniture at all? Not even a bed to sleep on?'

'They must have slept on the floor last night,' Maura said. 'All they seem to have is a few saucepans and the clothes on their backs.'

'But that's terrible!' Mammy said.

'Himself said to me this morning that he was hoping to get a couple of beds out of the stores in the Barracks today. When I was talking to Mrs Tynan later on she told me they might be able to get a table and a few chairs as well.'

'I don't know what to say at all,' Mammy was shaking her head in disbelief. 'God help that woman trying to mind those children in a place like that.'

'I'll have to go,' Maura said, 'or my crowd will be meeting me halfway out the Line, shouting for their tea.' She said goodbye to me as if I were an adult, and I said goodbye to her. She stepped out of the kitchen with my mother. Jacky scurried along at Mammy's side, clapping his hands in a rhythmic beat. I heard the clanking of cans from the hall, and then the exchange of goodbyes between Mammy and Maura. In a moment she passed the window, walking stiff-backed with short, energetic steps, carrying her cans of swill.

After she had gone through the Gate she would turn right and walk in the shadow of the Barracks wall for about a hundred yards; then she would clamber carefully between two strands of a wire fence, taking care not to spill her hard-won cargo, and negotiate the narrow, bumpy track down the railway embankment to the Line. I could see her in my mind, hauling her cans in the dusk along the Line, until she reached the low wall that separated the railway line from the curving shoreline where she lived. When she crossed that wall she'd be standing beside the old Schoolhouse where that other family lived now, hoping for beds and chairs and a table. I shivered, looking out the window at the darkening Barracks.

'They'll be warm anyway.' My mother's voice brought me back. Her hand rested for an instant on my shoulder and I looked up to meet her gaze. I had given up trying to figure out how she always seemed to know what was going through my head. 'Maura told me out in the hall that the fireplace and the chimney in the old School are working all right, and she told them they could take some turf out of her yard.'

'I hope they get the beds and stuff,' I said to her.

'I'm sure they will,' Mammy said. 'Sure God is good.'

They changed the rules about drawing turf from the turfyard.

You could never tell the reason for such changes in the rules. One day it might be perfectly legal to go to the canteen if you had the price of a bar of chocolate in your pocket; the next day the canteen might be out of bounds. In any case, it didn't occur to you to ask for reasons. What was allowed yesterday was forbidden today: your father announced it at the table, maybe at teatime or at dinnertime when you were breathless from running from the midday bus. Sometimes it was your mother who announced these changes in the regulations: 'Your Daddy told me that . . .' And when she had finished with the announcement of the new prohibition or amended dispensation, she'd say: 'Let ye not forget now what I'm after tellin' ye, I don't want ye to be gettin' into any trouble.' Rules and regulations were made by other people who didn't live in the Married Quarters.

The announcement about the turf was like that. One day it was forbidden for us to take turf from the turfyard (although it was not unknown for a friendly soldier to leave a bag of turf standing behind the hall door) and the next we were allowed to do so.

The turfyard occupied a large plateau of ground just outside the eastern wall of the Barracks. Three sides of the yard were surrounded by ten-foot-high fencing – tautly drawn strands of bullwire with barbs savage enough to tear your trousers or draw blood from unwary flesh at the slightest contact. The strands of bullwire were strung too closely together for anyone to slip between them. Climbing over the fence was even more daunting: at the very top, strong batons of wood angled outwards from the upright stakes, and these batons carried yet more strands of the wicked bullwire. You might, with luck, climb unbloodied to the top of the fence but these topmost angled rows of bullwire made it impossible to throw your leg over. The fourth side of the turfyard was the Barracks wall itself.

The turf was delivered from the bogs in high lorries with wooden sides. They drove along the tarred road above the Line (the short road that Maura walked with her cans before negotiating the downward slope to the railway tracks) and passed through the high, bullwire-laden gates that were flung open during the day. Some of the turf was stacked in reeks out in the open air. More of it was stored in a tall shed, higher even than the Barracks wall, to keep it dry.

There always seemed to be a few soldiers, usually recruits, at work in the turfyard, and they were tolerant enough whenever we ventured into the shed to play cowboys and Indians or cops and robbers. Getting a foothold on the stacked turf could be perilous, but that spiced the thrill of the ascent to the very top, until you stood at the summit of the black-brown mountain and you could touch the rusted galvanised roof with your fingertips. You were sure of a lecture when you got home, your hair matted with turf-mould, but sometimes one of the recruits would let you fill a sandbag with small, hard *ciarans*, and you knew that your precious booty would stall any complaints as surely as the cavalry headed off marauding redskins at the canyon.

And then one day it was legal to draw turf for the Quarters from the turfyard.

Art and myself hurried homewards along the Line after school that day. We'd heard the news at dinnertime. 'Ye're allowed to bring turf out of the turfyard,' Mammy had said, putting the plate of mashed potatoes and boiled turnips in front of me. 'Don't dilly-dally after school on the way home.' The snag was that the gates of the turfyard were closed and bolted soon after four o'clock, in anticipation of the Barracks closing down for the day at half past four. School didn't end until three-thirty.

Art and I were a long way clear of the other lads. When we paused to draw breath on the middle bridge we could see, behind us, Bobby, Tommy and Paul walking across Lough Atalia bridge. My face was wet with perspiration from our dash through the streets of town and up over the Bandroom hill. I flexed my shoulders to ease the chafing straps of my school-bag and I felt the sweat trickling down my back. In the windblown chill of the afternoon my body was on fire from my exertions.

'Better rest our horses awhile,' Art puffed. I nodded and we both dismounted, loosely tethering our horses to the top bar of the bridge. The tide was out: the sands stretched dull and grey under the banks of clouds, and a thin wisp of smoke curled upwards from the chimney of the old fever hospital in the near disance. 'More nesters,' Art said, pointing with outstretched hand at the trail of smoke. 'Soon they'll have the whole West fenced in and there'll be no prairies left.'

Our 'prairies' reached from the railway-causeway to the shore-line: the gorse-covered boggy expanse of the Furze. Sometimes these wetlands were our Black Hills of Dakota, or maybe the wilds of Wyoming; today, in the aftermath of an elegiac Buck Jones tale of a Wild West being fenced-in by advancing sod-busters, it was the shrinking prairies. The telltale smoke told of new settlers: all of us in the Quarters knew that the old fever hospital – a grim building set on a rocky corner of the Furze across from the docks, where diseased sailors were once interned – had been broken into by an old civvy and his family. More than once we'd seen the old fellow and his wife carrying their bags of messages across the Furze to the old hospital.

'Must be cold for them down there,' Art said, his gaze fixed upon the grey building. 'And my father said they probably have rats in it from the docks.'

For the moment our tethered horses were forgotten before the more vital reality of empty grates and freezing hands. 'Let's hit the trail,' I said, 'or the trading post might be closed.'

We saddled up and Art swung round in the saddle. 'That gosh-darned posse is getting too close for comfort,' he said, pointing back at the others who were gaining on us. 'Time to move out.'

We moved out and homewards along the Line, desperadoes now, fleeing from the marshal and his posse. Our horses' hooves thundered across the wooden planks of Paddy Walsh's bridge, and within moments we were labouring up the chapel hill. Finally we breasted the hill, puffing and blowing, outside the Barracks gates. When we looked back from our vantage-point we could see the others, tiny in the distance, halfway along the Line.

'Let's get the gold,' I said to Art. We ran helter-skelter into the barracks, not even breaking stride as we shouted hello to Paul O'Dowd's father, who was on duty at the Gate. 'See you in two shakes!' I shouted to Art, hurrying down the steps that led to the Quarters, while Art hared around the corner of the block to Number 1.

'At the steps,' he shouted back, 'with the bags!'

There was neither time nor breath for further words. My studded boots rang out on the stone hallway of Number 2. Mammy was sitting in front of the fire in the kitchen, feeding the baby her bottle.

'I'm back!' I shouted, unbuckling my school-bag from my back and dumping it in a corner of the kitchen. 'And I'm off again for the turf – Art is waiting for me!' Into the scullery then, grabbing the sandbag from where I'd left it folded beside the coaltub. Steel studs ringing again on the hall as I dashed out to meet Art.

'Kevin!' I could hear my mother calling after me, but I ignored her: time was of the essence.

Art was already waiting for me at the top of the steps, his sandbag folded under his arm. When he turned to greet me his features were crinkled up with laughter inside the circle of his balaclava. 'Um new wagon-train,' he said, laughing and pointing towards the gate. A uniformed soldier was coming towards us at a trot, pushing a low-slung, long-handled carriage that sat on two wheels the size of bicycle wheels. The carriage was piled high with sods of turf and on top of the pile, grinning from ear to ear, sat my brother Jacky with his arms raised like a parading conqueror in his chariot.

'What is it?' I gasped.

'It's a fancy pram!' the soldier yelled. 'A fancy pram for carrying turf and little soldiers!'

'A fancy pram!' Jacky shouted, drumming his heels on the heaped-up turf.

'It's a mortar-shell carriage,' Paul O'Dowd announced. He and the other lads had just arrived and were now gathered around the turf-laden contraption with Art and myself.

'Maybe it was that in the ancient Irish army,' John Lovett said – I recognised John now, the unmarried company sergeant who was a friend of my father's – 'but in the modern army it's a fancy pram and that's that!' He braced himself against the crossbar of the long handle and shouted at my brother: 'Steady yourself, young fella, we're off again!'

Jacky shouted, 'We're off!' and the soldier pushed, and the carriage gathered momentum, speeding away from us. Bemused, the rest of us watched the bent, receding back of the soldier. Jacky was hidden from our view, but his shouts of delight came back to us like Indian war-whoops across the plains. We watched the fancy pram's helter-skelter progress with envy: a latter-day wagon-train racing at full tilt along the Old Chisum Trail while frightened Redskins scattered in dismay on all sides. At the far end of the Quarters the fancy pram disappeared briefly from view as John Lovett negotiated the angle that led back up again inside the wall which separated the Quarters from the rest of the Barracks.

When it reappeared, there were two small figures propped up on top of the carriage full of turf. 'Who else is in the fancy pram?' Art asked. Already a new phrase had become an essential part of our everyday vocabulary.

'It's the small guy from the new crowd,' Paul said. He gazed out from under the level palm of his left hand, like the naval captain we'd seen in a film.

'Peter Tynan,' I said, recognising the boy perched behind my brother, as the fancy pram careered closer to us.

'The turf must be for your house,' Bobby said to me, and just then the fancy pram drew to a halt outside the door of Number 2. Jacky and his new pal, Peter Tynan, clambered down noisily. From our vantage-point on top of the steps we watched with mature silence.

John Lovett looked up towards us. He had his tunic off and his outstretched arms were laden with sods of turf. 'Don't be standin' up there lookin' at us!' he called out. 'Give us a hand and then we'll draw turf for the rest of ye!' Almost as one we bolted down the steps and gathered round the high-wheeled carriage. 'Take an

113

armload apiece,' John ordered, 'and then we can draw another few loads from the yard.'

We needed no second telling. Within minutes the entire load of turf was stacked beside the coal-tub in our scullery and we gathered expectantly around the now-empty fancy pram.

John Lovett looked at our eager, red-cheeked faces and laughed. 'I know what ye fellows want,' he joked, 'but it isn't a bus I have here and anyway I couldn't push the whole lot of ye together.' A disappointed silence settled upon us as we studied the empty carriage. Metal struts ran across the base of its boat-like interior. 'I think,' John Lovett said, 'that I could only give a spin to two or three of ye at a time.'

Pandemonium broke loose. Everybody wanted to be first and nobody wanted to wait. The din of shouting drew my mother to the door to see what was going on.

'Q-U-I-E-T!' John Lovett's roar silenced us. 'They're worse than a crowd of hungry recruits shoutin' for their dinner,' he said to my mother.

'Thanks for the turf,' Mammy said, laughing at him. 'Come in for a cuppa tea when you're finished. I've an apple tart just out of the oven.'

'I will, Missus,' he said, 'and thanks very much.' He looked up at the darkening sky. 'It must be nearly time for the turfyard to close – I doubt we'll get more than one more load.' He turned again towards us. 'I'll take three of ye in the pram,' he said, 'and the rest of ye will have to push.' We waited, breathless, as his gaze swept across us. 'You, you and you' – I was the last one pointed to – 'into the pram. Now, let the rest of ye push!'

Bobby, Art and I tried to balance ourselves in the curved base of the fancy pram. John Lovett had the crossbar of the long handle gripped in both his hands and the veins stood out on his forehead as he pushed us along. Tommy and Paul raced alongside us, one on either side of the fancy pram. Coming back, it would be their turn to sit on top of the turf.

My mother stood on the doorstep of Number 2 as we pulled away. My brother Jacky stood to one side of her, waving frantically after us. On the other side of her stood Peter Tynan. He was the same age as Jacky, but he was thinner, and he sometimes looked at you through his glasses as if he had lost his way. I waved to them all as we hurtled across the rough surface in front of the Quarters, and they waved back. My mother's arm dropped and I watched her instinctively draw Peter to her side and I was glad that his family had got a home in the Quarters and that they no longer lived in the old Schoolhouse beside the railway tracks. Peter and his family were home now: they had found a place where they belonged.

Joe came in with the milk every day. You'd hear him before you saw him, his approach heralded by the rhythmic drumming of his pony's hooves on the tarred barracks surface. The pony's grey-white coat always shone lustrously; his long mane flew like dappled plumes in the wind. By contrast, Joe himself seemed not half so clean. His shirt might once have been white, but you wouldn't want to bet on it; grubby and collarless, it flapped open at his powerful neck to reveal a sprouting of downy, ginger hair. The same fuzzy hair escaped from his reddish ears and flaring nostrils, but his round face was hairless. Even the backs of his hands, veined like mountain ridges, were gloved with the same ginger down. It was as if nature had played a joke on Joe; among ourselves we often speculated about the hairiness of his back.

But you'd never joke about Joe's driving of his pony and trap. He sat back in one corner of the trap, the long reins resting loosely in his hairy hands. Often when he'd given me a spin in the trap I'd watched those hands at work – a touch this way and the pony turned, a flick there and the animal accelerated, slowed or stopped. He never shouted at the pony: you'd think you heard a murmuring on the wind, like the rosary coming from an open window that you were passing, and when you cocked your ear you'd realise it was Joe talking under his breath to his grey-white pony. You'd see the animal prick his ears, pink-white and tender as a cat's, and then his movements would answer his master's muted instructions.

You'd think the trap was too fragile to bear the combined weight of Joe and the two churns of milk. It was a two-wheeled carriage of fine dark wood, curved along the front and sides, with a shelf-like flat piece that extended out over each wheel. The rear of the trap had a small door that opened outwards; below the doorway was a single step. When you stepped up into the trap, it seemed to tilt backwards towards you, and you moved quickly to take your place on one of the narrow seats on either side of the carriage.

In the small floor space between the seats stood Joe's two milk churns – yard-high, grey metal containers with wide-necked lids that slotted down inside the necks of the churns. Two measuring cups hung from two hooks inside the trap – a pint measure and a quart measure. Not that the measures were really necessary. When Joe's trap drew to a halt in the space outside the armourer's shop – right opposite the door of Number 2 – the women of the Quarters sent the children over with jugs that were either pint or quart vessels. Joe measured out the milk anyway. He lifted the lid from the churn and you could smell the warm milk inside before you saw it, rich and frothy and creamy. He took the measure in his calloused hand, dipped it into the foaming liquid and poured it into the jug that you held out in readiness. You waited for the extra drop. 'And an extra drop for yourself,' he always said, topping up your jug to the brim.

It was a ritual, like pouring from the cruets of water and wine into the chalice at Mass. Sometimes the milk spilled over Joe's horny fingers but there was no napkin to dry them, as there was to dry the priest's fingers when you poured water over them into the chalice. Joe wiped his fingers on his black trousers. Sometimes he pinched the tufts that grew from his nostrils between thumb and forefinger before cleaning them also on his black trousers.

Joe shouted at you to make a queue for the milk. 'Line up properly,' he'd shout, 'or ye'll frighten the pony and spill the milk.' The pony stayed still while we went on jostling for position. The pushing was half-hearted: nobody would wilfully break a jug that belonged to somebody else. Neither would anybody deliberately spill someone else's milk, although the small kids stumbled sometimes, particularly those making the long hike up the steps in the Arch to their homes on the veranda. Jugs broken or milk spilt, it was all money, and there was no one among us who didn't realise that.

Money was very much on my mind right now, queuing up with the other kids. Art was narrating a new Kit Carson epic, one I hadn't yet read, but for once the magic of the great plains failed to capture my interest.

One of the smaller kids from upstairs on the veranda tried to burrow past me in the queue, his jug enveloped by both arms against his chest, but Art caught him by the neck of his jumper and pulled him back. 'Get back in the queue, smartypants,' Art told him. 'Only for you're so small, I'd wring your neck for claim-jumpin'.'

The small fellow squirmed in Art's grip. 'Let go of me,' he protested. 'Anyway, I was five last week!'

'I'm eight next month,' Art said mildly, 'so just behave yourself.' His captive began to splutter further protestations.

'Be quiet, Sutton,' I said, 'or Art and myself will feed you to the alligators.' The boy shook himself as Art released his grip. 'And no telling tales to my mother,' I said. 'You shouldn't be jumping the queue anyway.'

He glared at Art and myself but he said nothing. He was a small, skinny fellow who suffered the indignity of having to wear multi-coloured pants that his mother knitted for him. They looked more like knickers than trousers. Sometimes when his mother was in our kitchen talking to Mammy, I had thought of sabotaging the next knitted trousers by stealing the ever-present knitting needles, but the opportunity never presented itself.

'What's up, pardner?' Art asked me. 'Got something on your mind?'

I leaned close to him and cupped my hand around his ear. 'It's my money-box,' I whispered. 'It's missing – I mean it *was* missing, but I found it today on the shelf in the scullery.'

Art drew back from me, horror written on his freckled face. 'The treasure,' he said, drawing close to me again, 'is the treasure gone?'

I nodded miserably. 'It was open,' I said, 'up on the shelf, behind the box with the polish brushes and stuff. I was after searching for it for days – I asked everybody, even Mammy – ' I bit my lip, unable to continue. Cry-baby tears would be out of place here, in the queue edging forward to Joe's trap. There were only two ahead of me now.

'Was it *all* gone?' Art whispered. 'The *whole* treasure?' The 'treasure' was my Communion money: eleven-and-sixpence stashed in my money-box – a black tin box decorated with red and yellow lines and a small brass handle. It looked like Long John Silver's treasure-chest.

The queue shuffled forward. Liam Bergin passed us carrying his quart jug with the apprehensive gait of a competitor in the egg-and-spoon race. Some smart aleck at the back shouted 'Boo!' at Liam, but he just laughed good-humouredly and went on his stiff-legged way.

'Was it *all* gone?' Art asked again.

'Everything except for two shillings,' I said. 'There was just a two-bob piece left in it, and it wasn't even locked.' I'd been stunned when I'd found the money-box. I'd searched the entire chest of drawers in our bedroom even though only the top drawer was mine. Miriam and Jacky had protested when I'd gone through the stuff in their drawers, but I was heedless of their protests. I'd spent a half-crown out of my Communion money, and two shillings of that went on the little black treasure-chest that caught my eye in the window of the Bargain Stores. I had stowed the locked box in my drawer and kept the silver key in my pocket. I wanted to cry out against the injustice of it all, seeing my treasure-chest there at the back of the scullery shelf, its lid ajar, its only contents the silver two-shilling piece.

'Any clues, Kevin? Any suspects?' For Art it was a puzzle. For me it was a disaster. There was a fat book in O'Gorman's that I coveted, but *Great Adventure Stories For Boys* was beyond me now, like the silver mouth organ that gleamed in the window of Raftery's.

'I don't know, Art,' I said. 'I just can't figure it out.' My brother Jacky had no use for money, and you couldn't doubt Miriam's denial of even knowing where the box had been hidden.

I was at the head of the queue now. I held out the jug with the blue stripes on it to Joe and I watched him fill the quart measure from the grey churn. It wasn't fair, but there was nothing I could do about it. Even Mammy had turned angrily on me. 'I don't want to hear another word about that money box,' she'd snapped. 'Haven't you two shillings for yourself anyway!'

'But I had eleven-and-six in it! What good is two bob!'

'Not another word out of you about it!' Mammy had said quietly. 'Not another word!' It was the quietness in her voice that silenced me. Mammy got cross sometimes, and shouted at you, but you always knew there was no real anger in her: a moment later the raised voice was forgotten. This was different, this absence of movement, like menace coiled. And it wasn't fair. It was money that I'd saved, that I hadn't spent as the other kids had done, on Corrib Orange and ice-cream and bars of chocolate.

'It's not fair,' I said under my breath.

'What's not fair, young fella?' Joe asked, handing me the jug of milk.

'Nothing.'

'Then it couldn't be less,' Joe grinned at me, the sprouts of red hair waving from his nostrils as his nose wrinkled. He reached into the inside pocket of his jacket and drew out a small brown envelope. 'Let you give that to your Mammy,' he said, handing me the envelope. 'Don't lose it now.'

'What is it?' I asked him.

'You know what curiosity did to the cat,' Joe said. 'Just give it to your mother like a good lad.'

My mother's name was scrawled in pencil on the grubby brown envelope. 'It's not very good handwriting,' I said, looking at it. 'The Brother at school would give you a few slaps for this.'

'God give me patience,' Joe said. 'It's no wonder I prefer to talk to me oul' pony – at least he doesn't give me any lip.'

'Give us a look,' Art said, peering over my shoulder.

'That's enough!' Joe roared, and the white pony, startled, shook himself between the shafts and the milk slopped in the heavy churns on the floor of the trap. 'Off with you now,' Joe said sternly, 'and be sure to hand that letter to your Mammy.'

Art and I winked at each other. 'Medicine man mad,' he muttered as I passed by, and I chuckled to myself.

The wind was rising, whipping the dust and grit into my face, and I covered the top of the jug with Joe's letter to keep the milk clean. The day was drawing to its close: rectangles of light from the Quarters windows splashed onto the veranda and the street outside the ground storey of the block. The wind darted with unseen tongues around the corner from Art's house and I held the letter more firmly on top of the jug. In the white light of the lamp at the corner of the Magazine it reminded me of the paten that the priest placed on top of the chalice after communion at Mass.

I was halfway down the steps to the Quarters when I heard Art calling me from behind. I didn't dare turn around: my eyes were focused firmly on the jug of milk. 'Keep your eyes peeled for bushwhackers!' Art shouted.

'And watch out – ' I lowered my left leg cautiously onto the next step ' – for rattlesnakes,' I answered.

'Fire one shot if you need help.' Art's voice was coming from the corner now, as he made his own careful way home, but I couldn't risk lifting my gaze from my envelope-covered jug.

'Meet you at the Arch after tea, pardner.'

The gravel crunched under my feet. Above my head now, and to my right, I could hear Joe declaring his old refrain. 'And a drop for yourself.' He was nearly finished now. Within minutes he'd lid the empty churns and take his seat in the corner of the trap, and he'd coax the white pony into action and we'd hear the clip-clopping of hooves echoing between the locked buildings of the Barracks. It was a lonesome sound that made you think of a friendless cowboy drinking his mug of coffee beside his small fire in the western wilderness.

I pushed in the heavy front door of Number 2. No light shone in the hallway, but I made my way with ease along the familiar passage. At the scullery door I stopped and carefully removed the envelope from the top of the jug. I pocketed the envelope and turned the brass knob. Across the last single pace of scullery darkness then, and I swung open the kitchen door.

My mother was standing beside my father's place at the far end of the table. She paused in pouring tea for him and looked across at me. 'Leave the milk on the table here beside your father,' she said, 'and go and warm yourself at the fire. You look frozen.'

I left the jug on the table and crossed the kitchen to stand in front of the range. I held my hands in front of the glowing bars and my fingers tingled in the heat.

'Use the fresh milk,' I heard my mother say to my father. 'You always like the fresh drop.'

I rubbed my hands together and flexed the fingers of my right hand. A frozen trigger-finger could prove fatal in a tight corner. 'I nearly forgot, Mammy,' I said abruptly. 'Joe gave me a letter for you.'

I took the letter from my trousers pocket and held it out to her. She took the letter from me without a word and slipped it into the pocket of her apron. 'Mammy!' I was surprised. 'Aren't you going to read the letter?'

'Sit over and have your tea,' she said to me. The sharpness in her voice hurt me.

'But Joe said – '

'Never mind what Joe said.' I was confused: I had done nothing to earn the rebuke. 'Now have your tea.'

I felt the tears pricking at the corners of my eyes as I took my place at the bottom of the table opposite my father.

He looked up from the racing page of the newspaper but I kept my eyes downward on the yellow oilcloth. 'What's in the letter from the milkman?' he asked.

You could hear the alarm clock ticking loudly on the mantelpiece while we waited for my mother's answer.

'Probably just the bill,' she said at length.

'I didn't know Joe sent bills around to the houses,' my father said.

'Sometimes he does.'

'How much is the bill?'

'Just the usual, I suppose.'

'Why don't you look at the bill to find out?'

I caught Miriam's eye as this exchange went on between my parents. I could feel in myself the alarm that I could read in her expression.

'Why don't you look at it?' my father repeated.

'Sure it's only the usual,' Mammy said.

'Show me the letter.'

'It's only the usual.'

'Give it to me,' my father said.

She looked at him for a moment and then, as if she had resigned herself to something, I saw her shoulders slump and she drew the crumpled envelope from the pocket of her apron and placed it in my father's outstretched hand. He ripped the envelope open with a harsh tearing sound. Nobody spoke while he unfolded the single sheet of paper and scanned its contents. I looked at my mother. Her eyes were fixed on my father's face. He looked up from the letter.

'How can it be so much?' he demanded. 'You mustn't have paid him for months.'

My mother said nothing: she just looked at him.

'Well? You owe the man over four pounds!'

I gulped nervously.

'I can't manage,' Mammy said.

'You get your money every week,' my father said.

'I can't manage on it,' Mammy said, 'I do my best but I can't manage.'

'You'll have to manage like everybody else.'

My mother was silent.

'Have you nothing to say for yourself?' my father asked.

Still she did not speak. She was motionless, perched on the edge of her chair like a bird that could not fly.

Abruptly my father stood up, pushing his armchair back noisily. He threw the crumpled sheet of paper on the kitchen table and grabbed his tunic from the back of the chair. We were all silent as he buttoned his tunic up to the neck: the soft swish of the tunic on the brass buttons was loud in the breathless kitchen. He flexed his powerful shoulders and pulled down the ends of the tunic so that it hung properly. Capless and beltless, he stood for a long moment at the end of the table before turning and crossing the kitchen. We waited for the door to slam, but he closed it quietly behind him.

Even when the ring of his boots on the stone floor of the hall could no longer be heard, even then, nobody at the table spoke.

As always, it was Miriam who knew what to do. She climbed noiselessly down from her chair and sidled nervously alongside the table until she stood beside her mother. 'Mammy?'

My mother still sat birdlike on the edge of the kitchen chair, her unseeing eyes fixed on some spot high up on the curtains. She gave no sign that she had heard my sister speak to her.

'Mammy?' This time Miriam reached out a finger to tap my mother's folded hands. With an effort that was obvious in the way she seemed to shake herself, my mother hauled herself back from that uncritical spot on the curtain and bent to speak to Miriam.

'What is it, *a ghrá*?' she asked, and her voice was weary, as though the journey from that place above my head had been long and exhausting.

'You can have this, Mammy,' Miriam said, holding out her upturned hand. From where I sat I could see the small English sixpence shining on her palm. And I could see the smile shining on Mammy's face.

'Keep your money, pet,' she said. She closed Miriam's fingers over the coin and drew my sister in close beside her, her hand still covering Miriam's. 'Where did you get all that money?' she asked.

'Did you rob a bank or something?' My mother's eyes were wide with mock-horror at the enormity of Miriam's supposed crime.

'I didn't rob a bank!' Miriam retorted. 'Only robbers do that!'

'Where did you get it then?' Mammy probed gently.

'Maura gave it to me when I helped her to carry the buckets as far as the Gate.'

'You're a great little girl,' my mother said to her. 'But you're to keep your own money for yourself.'

I was fingering my two-shilling piece in my pocket but the moment for a heroic offering was past now. To offer my money now would be sham-heroism, knowing for sure that my mother would tell me to keep it. The moment was Miriam's, and I couldn't find it in my heart to envy her.

'But the money for the milk,' Miriam said quietly. 'Daddy said – '

'Never mind that!' The vehemence with which Mammy cut off Miriam's words surprised me. 'Don't you worry yourself about that,' she went on, more gently now. Abruptly she stood up and took Miriam's hands in hers. 'In fact the two of us are going over to the canteen this very very minute, just the two of us, and you can buy yourself a bar of chocolate.'

'Just you and me?' Miriam's eyes twinkled.

Mammy nodded. 'Just you and me.'

'Can I come too?' Jacky asked.

'Not this time,' Mammy said, and there was a lilt of gaiety in her voice. 'No boys this time – just the ladies!'

'I'll get the coats, Mammy!' Miriam said. She almost danced across the kitchen and out into the scullery. Within seconds she was back, breathless and bright-eyed, nearly weighed down by the burden of the two coats.

I watched silently as Mammy helped Miriam into her coat and buttoned it up for her. Then she put on her coat and took Miriam's hand in hers. 'Now,' she said brightly, 'the ladies can go out to do their shopping.' At the kitchen door Mammy turned and spoke to me. 'Keep an eye on the small ones, we'll be back in a few minutes.'

I waited until I heard the outside door closing before I reached out for the crumpled sheet of paper that had come to rest against the jug on the table. I moved my mug to one side and laid the paper on top of the oilcloth. My father had crumpled it badly in his fist. I had to smooth it over and over with the edge of my hand to make the paper lie flat on the table.

'I'm telling Mammy that you're reading the letter,' Jacky said.

I ignored him. The note was written in pencil on the faint blue lines of the small page. The quality of writing would merit a substantial number of slaps at school.

Dear Mrs Brophy, Joe had written, *I regret that I have to remind you again that you have not paid me for the milk for some time. The amount is £4–2–6. I will need some payment this week. I hope you and your family are keeping well.*

He had written 'Yours faithfully' above a signature which was indecipherable. I had to read it slowly to make out the words, and then I read it again.

'What's in the letter?' Jacky asked me.

I didn't ignore him this time. 'Nothing good,' I said quietly.

'Is that why Mammy is sad?'

'That's why,' I said. She hadn't fooled Jacky either, putting on her coat and brushing her hair and taking Miriam by the hand to spend her sixpence in the canteen.

'When I'm big,' Jacky said, 'I'm going to get tons of money for Mammy.' I smiled across the table at him. 'I am!' he insisted. 'Tons and tons of half-crowns and sixpences and everything!'

'I know,' I said.

'Tons of half-crowns!' he repeated.

You'll have to wait your turn, I thought to myself, I'll give them to her first. Never again, when I was grown-up, would she have to borrow from a small black money-box and then leave the nearly empty treasure chest on the shelf in the scullery. I squirmed in my chair, recalling with shame how I had questioned her about my eleven-and-sixpence and the uncharacteristic way in which she had hushed me. The pioneers of the Wild West had searched for the secret trails across the mountains until they stumbled gratefully into the green lands of plenty – and so would I, I told myself, so would I.

I looked up from Joe's letter and spoke to Jacky. 'There'll be tons of half-crowns for us all,' I said, and my brother smiled back at me.

EIGHT

John Joe Hartigan was on his feet, labouring over the spelling of the word 'beauty'. Twice he had stumbled as far as the second letter. 'B-E-'

Now he fell back again to the safety of the first letter. 'B-'

'That's the third time you've started,' Brother Edmond said mildly, 'and we're all agreed that the word begins with the letter B.' Our teacher's mild tone deceived no one, least of all John Joe. His tall, narrow body leaned backwards, as if he wished to escape from the confines of the long classroom bench, but he was trapped awkwardly between the writing top of the desk and the plank-like seat which chafed against the backs of your knees when you stood up to answer a question.

Brother Edmond's eyes were not as soft as his words. His gaze was fixed upon the unhappy John Joe, seemingly pinned as firmly to the second letter of the word as he was within the cage of his desk. We were all aware of John Joe's dilemma. You were permitted an uncertain amount of shuffling backwards and forwards between letters that were *not* incorrect, but to utter an incorrect letter was to signal an end to your efforts. Stumbling your way through spelling a word was like trying to negotiate a passage through a minefield: you put each foot down gingerly on the treacherous soil, and you savoured the relief of continued survival, yet always there was that grim warmonger on the sidelines, pushing you deeper and deeper into the mine-infested terrain.

We could hear John Joe's loud breathing, raspy in the quiet classroom. He squirmed in the narrow space of the desk, turning sideways so that his haunted face was clearly visible to those of us sitting in the last desk. He had a strange face, narrow and flat, as if his mother had accidentally ironed his face while she was ironing the shirts at home in Bohermore.

'Get a move on, John Joe,' Brother Edmond said, even more mildly, 'or we'll be here all night. Don't you want to go home at all today?'

Nobody smiled at the Brother's sally. Ten minutes more would see an end to a long day. To John Joe it must have seemed ten years away. You had to feel sorry for him – reading and spelling in either English or Irish were a perpetual mystery to John Joe. Sometimes you'd see him in a corner of the yard during the break with his English book open at the page for spellings and his eyes closed while his lips silently mouthed the letters of the difficult words. They were all difficult to John Joe. Which was just as well, since whichever team won the spelling contest would have no homework that night. No sums, no Irish or English writing: a whole evening free to play around the Barracks and finish off with the new 64-page Buck Jones beside the fire in the kitchen. Fingers plucked at my sleeve and I was aware of Paul O'Dowd leaning slightly towards me. 'If he doesn't get it,' Paul whispered out of the side of his mouth, 'nobody can catch up on us.'

I barely nodded my head: Brother Edmond had X-ray vision that equalled Superman's. Anyway, I'd worked it out for myself. It wasn't too hard to work out. If John Joe missed, then the Bohermore team, like the other teams, would fall two points behind us, while only one member of each team was left to answer his spelling. The last desk, made up mainly of Barracks lads, would have held its collective breath had it been somebody other than John Joe who was attempting to spell the word 'beauty'. Instead, we watched with an indifference that was only slightly tempered with sympathy. The night without homework was ours.

John Joe cleared his throat and harrumphed in his own characteristic way, so that we knew he was about to launch himself at do-or-die speed through the perils of the minefield. 'BUETY.'

Brother Edmond shook his head, as if more in sadness than in anger. He picked up the crook-handled bamboo cane from where it hung on the easel, below the blackboard, and advanced down the aisle of the classroom towards John Joe.

'B-U-double E-T-Y,' John Joe blustered.

'Wrong,' Brother Edmond said. 'Hold it out.' This was the other side of the classroom competition. You did your best not only to win the point for your team, but also to escape the punishment that went with failure. 'Hold it out,' the Brother repeated.

Like a lot of us, John Joe liked to take it on his left hand. He stretched out his left arm, and the Brother's cane flashed briefly before descending on John Joe's upturned palm. Brother Edmond waited while John Joe clenched and unclenched the fingers of the beaten hand. Once more he held out his left palm. When you had only two slaps coming to you, it was better to take them both on the same hand. That way you had at least one hand that didn't sting like fire.

John Joe and Brother Edmond stared impassively at each other for a moment, like boxers who have completed a savage round of fighting, but afterwards bear no malice towards each other. It was a rare day at school on which John Joe's hands did not feel the cut of the hooked cane, yet he never complained or appeared to resent it. A year or two older than the rest of us, he regularly held out his hand to embrace the just reward of his slowness at calculation, reading and spelling. He sat down quietly on the long bench, shaking his stinging hand as if it did not belong to the rest of him. I watched his swinging hand, the beaten fingers whirling like flying sausages, and I trembled inwardly, imagining the stabbing pain. Schoolwork came easily to me, so that I was rarely slapped, but on a couple of occasions I had felt the whiplash of the cane on my fingers for the misdemeanours of daydreaming, inattentiveness or talking in class. I could bear the imagined rigours of pioneer life in the Wild West far more easily than the sensation of the cane on my hand. It made John Joe's stoicism all the more remarkable to me.

The spelling contest was effectively over, but Brother Edmond completed the last round of questions for the remaining member of each team. The words he selected were not difficult: he seemed reluctant to create a situation in which the cane would have to be used again. An unspoken truce had been declared for the final minutes of the day. When he had finished the last round of questions he went through the ritual of totalling the marks for each team, but we were ahead of him.

'The Barracks won, Brother!' we dared to shout, confident that our raised voices would incur no wrath.

He smiled when he turned from the blackboard to face the class.

His teeth were white and even in his ruddy-complexioned face. 'The Barracks wins again!' Brother Edmond said beaming.

'The Barracks lads are the best, Brother!' Art called out triumphantly.

'Now,' the Brother admonished, 'no boasting! It was a close shave. Ye only won by a couple of marks in the end.'

'But we *are* the best, Brother!' Art persisted. 'Sure don't we win loads of times!'

'Ye didn't win last week,' Paul Cleary blurted out. Paul lived in Shantalla, a part of the town that was completely unknown to any of us from the Barracks. He had a quick brain and excelled at what we called 'mentlers' – arithmetic problems that you had to work out in your head. Now he swivelled in his desk in the middle row and wrinkled his nose at us. 'Shantalla won last week,' he said, 'are ye forgetting that?'

'Yeah, don't forget that!' Mike from Bohermore blurted out. 'Ye didn't win last week!'

'Well, we're better than Bohermore anyway!' Paul O'Dowd retorted.

'Sure anybody is better than stupid oul' Bohermore!' Tommy McDonagh added.

'Watch it, McDonagh!' Mike said menacingly. Despite his small-ness, Mike had a reputation for pugnacity.

'Are you going to make me?' Tommy asked. 'You and who else?'

'*That's enough!*' Brother Edmond's roar brought us back to the reality of the classroom. In the hushed silence that followed he rapped the crook of the cane on the blackboard. 'I've never heard such a carry-on!' he said quietly. 'I've a good mind to let nobody off lessons tonight!'

'Ah, Brother, that's not fair – ' Art's protest was abruptly cut off by the sound of the cane thudding thunderously on the front desk.

'I'll overlook that interruption, Art,' the Brother said, 'but only this once.'

We could tell that he wasn't really cross from the tone of his words. You could only go so far with Brother Edmond, but nobody among us would swap him for any of the other teachers in the school. He often stood with us on the sideline of the army playing-field below the Barracks, when the soldiers' hurling team was playing against a visiting side and once I'd seen him talking to

Mammy there when she'd come out to watch my father play for the barracks. 'Brother Edmond told me you're doing well at school,' she'd told me afterwards, but then refused to elaborate on what else had been said. 'Sure you'd only get a swelled head if I told you any more,' she'd tantalised me.

'Put the books away – *quietly!* – and we'll stand for the prayers.'

We put the books into our school-bags and closed the straps. We hooked our arms through the leather loops, hoisting the bags up on our backs, and fastened the clasp in front. Then we stood to say the final prayers of the day.

Minutes later we were streaming down the gravelled path that led to the street. The school buildings made up a square that surrounded a small lawn. Two sides of the square housed the Brothers' living quarters: whatever lay behind the brown door that led into this area could not even be imagined. The classrooms were contained in the rest of the grey, ancient buildings. Ceilings were high, floors creaked and in winter the icy wind from the river insinuated itself around the ancient windows. I knew the names of two other schools in the town – the Brothers themselves ran another primary school which I had never ever seen – but the Mon was the only place that mattered, as crucial to my existence as the Barracks itself.

We spilled out onto the street, beside the house where the priests lived, in gangs that corresponded roughly with the teams of Brother Edmond's spelling contest. Paul Cleary and his pals from Shantalla turned right at the gate: where Shantalla was, we had no idea. Its location, in any case was unimportant, being irrelevant to our lives. The boys from the town, 'the townies', were a less cohesive unit – their homes were scattered all over the central streets of the town. Some turned right, some took the left route, while a few of them crossed the road into the lane that led down by O'Gorman's bookshop *en route* to yet another lane which took them to their homes by the docks. These lads from the town lacked the sense of togetherness which so animated the teams from the Barracks, from Shantalla and from Bohermore in all our competitions.

Our gang from the Barracks gathered in a protective huddle outside the school gate. 'Redskins on the warpath,' Art said.

Mike and the other Bohermore fellows were lined up on the footpath opposite us. Although he was the smallest of the bunch, it was around Mike that the others clustered. John Joe stood at the back of the gang, his sad face staring solemnly at us across Mike's close-cropped head. Older and bigger than any of us, John Joe had never been known to lay a finger on anybody: his presence did not lend even moral sanction to the gang across the road, since everybody knew that he wouldn't fight. Even so, we all took good care never to push him too far – just in case.

Mike stepped forward a pace to the edge of the footpath. 'Have you anything to say about Bohermore now, McDonagh?' he shouted across the road.

Tommy's face grew red with anger as he also stepped to the edge of the pavement to shout back his defence. 'The Barracks fellows can always beat stupid oul' – '

'Wait!' It was Art who interrupted Tommy, pulling at the sleeve of his lumber-jacket.

Tommy rounded impatiently on Art. 'Wait for what?' he demanded. 'I'm not going to let your man tell me to shut up!'

'Easy, pardner, easy,' Art said soothingly. 'It's just that we're outnumbered – count for yourself.'

It was true. There were nine of them against our five.

Tommy shrugged. 'Any guy from the Barracks can handle two from Bohermore,' he said.

'Maybe not,' Art said. He looked at John, but said no more. Nor did I: my insides were turning to jelly at the prospect of being tackled by two of our enemies.

'What have you got to say?' Mike shouted. 'Are you all just a bunch of cowards now when the Brother isn't here!'

'We have to pow-wow!' Art called out.

'What'll we do?' I asked, trying to keep the trembling out of my voice.

'We could do a cavalry charge,' Tommy said, 'and take them by surprise. I mean, we'd be past them and up as far as the Line before they knew what happened.'

While our council of war was proceeding, other classes came out in droves from the school. They gave our two opposing factions plenty of breathing space: confrontations between gangs were a regular feature of life at the Mon. Most of them headed off home; a few stood by to see what might develop.

'Have you finished your stupid pow-wow?' Mike roared.

'Let's charge them,' Tommy said again.

130

'It won't work,' I said. 'It's too far to reach the Line – they'd catch us on Shop Street or around the Square.' I didn't add that Paul wouldn't make it around the corner before one of the Bohermore fellows got hold of him.

'Then we'll have to make peace,' Art said, 'there's nothing else for it.'

'I'm not making peace with that shower!' Tommy protested.

'We can break the peace when the signs are more favourable.' It was Paul's first contribution to the debate on the footpath, spoken in his usual deadpan manner, like the wireless announcer reading the racing results from Pontefract. We all smiled. Paul blushed.

'When the signs are more favourable,' Tommy repeated.

'Wait!' I said, remembering the various treaties that Kit Carson had brokered between the white man and the redskin. 'We cannot speak with a forked tongue.'

'We have to make peace,' Art said quickly, 'and the Barracks fellows always speak with a straight tongue.' He stepped off the pavement into the road.

'Are you looking for man-to-man stuff?' Mike called out to him, throwing his school-bag to the ground.

Art raised his hand above his head, palm outwards. 'We wish to make peace with our brothers from Bohermore,' Art announced solemnly.

Mike was nonplussed by this development. 'What d'you mean – peace?' he blustered. 'McDonagh said Bohermore guys are stupid!' He pointed accusingly at Tommy, standing beside me.

'They are stupid!' Tommy said, but under his breath.

Paul O'Dowd coughed loudly, and we all waited for him to speak. 'The words were spoken in the heat of the moment,' Paul said, 'and no offence was intended.'

Silence settled on the road. Peace was imminent, but all of us, on both sides, knew that honour demanded that Tommy should speak. 'No offence was intended!' he called out breezily.

Honour was satisfied. We watched Mike unclench his fists. 'Then we'll shake on it!' he said, smiling. He stepped out into the middle of the road and shook hands with Art. Then he crossed the street and stood looking at Tommy. 'Shake!' he said, holding out his hand. While Mike and Tommy were shaking hands, I noticed John Joe loping alone towards the corner, his brown school-bag bouncing on his back. The other Bohermore lads waited for us to cross the road. Normality was restored. Together we headed homewards.

The streets of our town were quiet. You could sometimes walk the length of Shop Street out in the middle of the road without having to give way to a motor car. We moved in a loose phalanx, voices raised, disagreement forgotten. We passed King's shop without pause, for nobody had a penny today to buy a bar. Mr King stood behind the high counter, looking gloomily out at us as we passed his door. He viewed the world through round, wire-rimmed spectacles. We figured they weren't very good glasses: once we passed off an American nickel as a shilling and walked away with two penny bars and tenpence change. In the summer months Mr King sold rabbits; you had to duck under their grey-brown stiff bodies hanging in the doorway to enter into the dark sanctum of the little shop. You always avoided their lifeless eyes when you came out with your penny bar.

Monaghan's shop was around the corner from King's, on the way to Shop Street. Whereas Mr King wore a brown shop coat and must be at least a hundred years old, Mr Monaghan always wore a collar-and-tie and was merely old like our parents. His round face had soft, glowing skin, and his hands were soft too. Mr Monaghan didn't smile when he handed you your bar or counted the ten marble sweets for a penny into your hand, but he wasn't cross either. His spectacles worked better than Mr King's: when we handed him an American coin he looked gravely at it before returning it with the hope that we hadn't accepted the coin as change in some other shop, since the coin was useless in Ireland. 'You'll have to go to America to spend that fellow,' Mr Monaghan said. He didn't smile when he said it, but you got the impression that inside he was having a great laugh at you. Today nobody went into Monaghan's shop, although we paused, just for a moment, to savour the array of juicy delicacies on display in the wide, deep window. The bars were displayed in rows of lidless boxes – Pixie bars, in their distinctive wrapper, dark brown like the hard toffee that you chewed into a succulent mess that dripped pleasure down your throat; Plug Tobacco's, and Cough-No-Mores, and marble sweets and conversation lozenges . . . There were sugar-coated bonbons and black and white bull's-eyes and liquorice pipes with red stuff on the bowl like spots of fire . . . It wasn't good to stand there too

long, just griggin' yourself, so we hurried by and turned into Shop
Street. Ahead lay Dillon's the jewellers, with the big clock overhead
and beside it the legend 'Dublin Time'. I never walked under it
without recalling my first day at school when I'd spelt out the two
words for Mammy, and how I'd asked her if Dublin time was
different from ours. I could smile a superior smile now, remembering how much of a little kid I'd been then. I was nearly grown up
now: in a few months I'd be ten and after the next summer holidays
I'd be passing into Fourth Class. At the corner of the Square we
parted from the other fellows: they went up the hill towards
Bohermore while we swung right in the direction of the railway
station and the Line.

Like Monaghan's window, the station held its own particular
treasures. The steps that led up and into the station were set in the
middle of a long grey building that stretched from the corner of the
Square to the foot of the Line. You passed the ticket-office and
stepped through the doorway onto the station platform. Sometimes
the ticket collector would be standing there, punching travellers'
tickets with his little hand-held machine, but today the entrance
was unguarded. Nor was there any train standing at the platform.
The great, vaulted hangar was empty and silent. Often we'd stood
enchanted by the ritual of departure – the slamming of doors, the
clouds of steam belching onto the platform, the whistle shrill above
the grunting engine and the guard's green flag waving as the train
clanked out and onwards to Dublin. Through the moving windows
we'd glimpse the unknown passengers opening newspapers, lighting
pipes or cigarettes, and we'd watch them pass and disappear without
curiosity: then we'd turn back to the real world, the treasures of
the station.

We stopped by the machine that printed your name on metal.
It was a heavy metal box, standing chest-high, the top sloping
towards you. Set in a circle on this top, like a clock-face, were the
letters of the alphabet and the figures 1 to 9. Unlike a clock, this
face had only one hand – a heavy, brass hand that you moved
around the letters to spell out your name. You had to put a
sixpenny bit into the machine to get the hand to move. You put
the sixpence in the slot, pressed it home and you were ready to go.
You moved the hand to the first letter of your name, pulled the
lever at the side, moved on to the next letter, and so on. You could

use the figures to print the number of your house in your address. The hand could also be moved to a spot on the face which said 'space', so that you could separate your words. The first time I'd used the machine I hadn't known about the space position, and the machine had pushed out a length of light grey metal which read 'KEVINTBROPHY2MARRIEDQUARTERSTHEBARRACKS'. The letters were punched into the strip of metal; when you turned the strip over, you could see the indentations. We had no American coins this evening; we tried a small washer that Bobby picked up from the platform, but it wouldn't fit into the money slot.

The football machine was our next stop. Two soccer teams, dressed in blue and red, were frozen forever in a glass case that sat on top of a heavy metal box. A goalkeeper stood at either end of the case, guarding his tiny net. In front of him were ranged his colleagues, stretching as far as the opposite goal in four rows of two, three, two and three. Every line was faced by a line of the opposing team. It took a shilling in the slot to bring out the white ball and start the game. Each player was rooted to his own spot: his right leg was hinged so that he could kick the ball, the movement controlled by small silver handles below the case. Sometimes the ball got stuck under a player's leg and you had to push and lift the entire heavy machine to release the ball. Our small metal washer wouldn't work in the football machine either.

'Hey! What're you fellows doin' there?' A station porter, having a smoke beside the station bookstall, was shouting at us.

'We're just winning the Cup final,' I called back to him.

'Well, shove off and win it up in the bloody Barracks,' he retorted.

We looked at one another, clustered around the machine. 'He must be from Bohermore as well,' Tommy said, and we all laughed.

Suddenly the Barracks seemed exactly the right place to be. Nobody said a word but, as one, we started to run towards home.

NINE

That summer I learned to swim.

It seemed no different from all my other summers. The long days of the holidays stretched endlessly ahead. School was not even a speck on the shimmering horizon, beyond the wide mouth of the bay, beyond the white lighthouse on its little island.

Breakfast was later than usual at Number 2: there was time to talk to Mammy while you drank your mug of tea and ate your slice of brown cake heaped with jam. You climbed out through the small window of the lavatory and unpegged your swimming togs from the clothes-line – all the lines of the Quarters billowed with drying clothes in the summer breeze – and, when you climbed back in, your mother handed you the white army towel, with your father's serial number stamped on it, and you said 'so long' to her and you headed down past the Married Quarters and out through the back gate of the Barracks, down across the sports fields (where sometimes the soldiers were practising manoeuvres) until you reached the Men's Side.

Women and girls were not allowed at the Men's Side. When you were just a young boy you went with your mother and the smaller children to the Beach Stores, at the other side of the sports fields, or even to the wide sweep of Ballyloughane, beside the old Schoolhouse that the Tynans had broken into. There your mother lighted a fire of twigs that you and the other children gathered, and she boiled the kettle of water that you'd carried from the Barracks, and she made tea that tasted better than it ever did at home, and you ate brown bread and currant cake that confirmed all over again your conviction that nobody baked better than Mammy. At the Beach Stores and at Ballyloughane your mother paddled in the water beside you, her skirt hitched up above her knees, and you played in the shallow water with Miriam and Jacky while the long afternoon drifted into languorous evening.

When you got older, the summer you were eight, you first headed for the Men's Side. Here was no place for infantile splashing and womanish fires and slices of cake. Sometimes the young soldiers horsed about on the grassy, sloping bank where you changed, sometimes they fought each other with wet swimming togs or dumped one another into the water, but they swam with confident strokes to the raft that floated far out, over their depth, and when they dived from the long board that edged out from the raft, they cut the water with the smoothness of a knife.

For two summers I'd watched them while I flailed in the shallows and wondered would I ever get the hang of it, would I ever power my way out to the bobbing raft and sit on its edge like a master of the waves, looking back at those stranded on the shore. Sometimes one of the soldiers would help me, placing his hand under my chin and my chest while I threshed with my arms, but when he released me, my frantic beating of the waters availed me nothing, and I tasted failure in salty mouthfuls. The raft bobbed in the summer haze like a distant dream.

That summer, the summer of my tenth birthday, Joseph came to the Men's Side. Joseph was old, so old that all his hair was grey. When he stripped and stood in his swimming togs his chest hung from him like a woman's, and he looked older than ever. Joseph was a civvy, one of the few civvies who walked half way out the Line and crossed over the Furze to swim at the Men's Side. Civvies did not undress and leave their gear on the sloping grassy bank where the soldiers did; they left their stuff on the big rocks at a respectful distance from the soldiers. Everyone knew that the civvies were here on sufferance in the army domain. We didn't mind, so long as they didn't take the best places on the sunny bank.

When Joseph hit the water, he ceased to be ancient. His body became young again, moving with the lazy ease of an athlete. All strokes came easily to him – overhand, breaststroke and backstroke. Sometimes he'd float on his back for ages, puffing contentedly on a cigarette while he stared at the summer sky. It was the cigarette in his mouth that attracted my attention, the first time I saw him wading into the water. I watched as he eased himself gently backwards into the water, the cigarette hanging from his lower lip. I watched him lie there on the water as if he belonged to it, while the smoke from his cigarette drifted upwards into the day. I edged across through the chest-high waters until I stood beside him.

'How come it doesn't get wet and go out?' I asked.

The grey head remained still in the water, but the faded blue eyes swivelled towards me. 'Minimum movement,' he said, and the lighted cigarette moved up and down as he spoke through barely opening lips. 'It's always minimum movement in the water.'

I could think of nothing else to say. I moved away but I kept an eye on him. When his cigarette was almost smoked he stood upright and I watched him flick the butt away abruptly with his index finger. Before the butt had hit the water he himself was launched silently into a powerful breaststroke that took him to the raft within seconds. I turned away and resumed my fruitless flailing. Sometimes I thought I'd got it: I'd manage three or even four frantic strokes but then once more the water closed over me and my feet were on the sandy floor.

'Minimum effort,' I heard beside me, as I surfaced, gasping from yet another unsuccessful attempt. The cigarette-smoking ancient civilian was standing beside me, his expression serious. 'You're making far too much movement,' he said to me. 'You're using up enough energy to swim out to the lighthouse.'

I hit the water with my fist in frustration. 'I'll never be able to swim,' I said sulkily.

The serious old face softened with a smile. 'You will,' he said, 'you will. Just remember – minimum movement and breathe deeply and regularly. Like this.' And he showed me, moving his fleshy arms in an easy overhand stroke, his hair-covered flabby upper body turning gently from side to side as he went through the motions.

'I know all that,' I protested. 'I just can't do it!'

'Sure you can do it,' he said cheerfully. 'You're just trying too hard. Try to move everything just a bit more slowly this time.' His optimism demanded that I should at least try. He winked at me, and I found myself smiling at him. 'Remember – minimum movement.'

I took a deep breath and eased myself down into the water, my left arm out in front, my right already bending into the overhead stroke. Gently, I told myself, gently. *Minimum movement.* I turned my head in the water and gulped for air. And then again. And repeat again. The water opened before me in a burst of heaving white and I knew I was swimming. The bay churned around my head but it was applause in my ears, the roar of success. When I stopped, fumbling with my feet for the sand, I leaped upwards from the water like a triumphant sea-beast. Through the blur of water in my eyes I could see Joseph, perhaps a dozen yards away, beaming at me. He raised his hand in acknowledgment and I waved back at him. 'I can do it! I can swim!'

'Well done,' he said quietly. He went on with his swimming.

The sun climbed higher in the summer sky and the soldiers on the bank gathered their things to go back to the Barracks for their midday meal. Dinner was the last thing on my mind. Throughout the long afternoon I crossed and recrossed the swimming area, bounded on either side by a line of grey pillars of stone. Once, when I looked towards the bank, I noticed that Art and the other lads had left, and I turned again to the sea as if it were the water of life. And once, when I looked out towards the bobbing raft, unmanned in the hazy afternoon, and I was about to launch myself towards its tantalising sanctuary, I felt Joseph's hand on my shoulder and he said, as if he could read my mind: 'Leave the raft for another day. Don't go out over your depth. Promise?'

I nodded. It was easy to postpone a dream, like saving half a Pixie bar in your pocket and pretending to yourself that you didn't have it. It was all the sweeter when you finally bit into the rich brown toffee.

Joseph left soon after that. He turned once, crossing the Furze towards the Line, and waved to me. I waved back, wondering idly where he lived. He wore a dark suit over a white shirt and tie, and his speech was gentler than the soldiers'. He grew smaller in the distance and then he climbed up the railway embankment to the Line and he was lost from view.

I stayed on, perfecting my stroke, trying and trying over again until I could cross the swimming area without stopping. When I finally made it across, I hauled myself exhausted onto the top of the pillars and sat there, gulping in great satisfied breaths, while the warm water washed over me. For a long time I sat there, savouring my triumph in the heat of the afternoon. The tide turned, ebbing away towards America on the other side of the world. More swimmers arrived – a few soldiers, a couple of civvies. I saw Seamus

Costello, the cook who lived on the veranda over Number 2, enter the water, dressed in his black army swimming togs. He stood in the shallows and stooped to dip his hand in the sea. Then he blessed himself with the salt water. You always did that when you went into the sea: you blessed yourself so that you wouldn't drown. He waded towards me. The tide was a long way out now: you had to wade a good distance to find deep water.

'Are you swimming out to the lighthouse, Seamus?' I asked him.

Seamus stood in the waist-high water with his arms folded across his chest. A heavy foliage of black hair matted his huge chest. His arms were as thick as my thighs. He considered my question seriously. Unlike many adults, Seamus always considered your questions carefully. 'I might go further today,' he said. 'I think that today I might go as far as Amerikay.' He smiled to show that he was making a joke, and then he was gone, the waters white in his wake. Seamus always swam the breaststroke. You'd think he was sliding down under the water, and then he'd surge upwards and forwards in an easy rhythm that seemed to swallow distance. I watched him pass the raft and then minutes later I could barely make out his head bobbing up and down in the water.

Seamus never spoke about his swims to the lighthouse, although everybody knew that he was the best swimmer in the Barracks. I wondered if Joseph could swim to the lighthouse. The lighthouse-keeper could give him a cigarette out there before he started on the long swim back to the Men's Side. Somehow I never got around to asking Joseph if he could swim to the lighthouse, although I saw him often at the Men's Side throughout that long summer of discovery. Perhaps that mattered much less than my own eventual and triumphant passage to the diving raft, where men rested and the children dared not follow. I never again saw Joseph after that summer of my tenth birthday.

I could see the small smile forming on Mammy's mouth as she read the letter. I was curious about the letter. Apart from the weekly cheques, there wasn't much for the postman to deliver to Number 2 or to any other house in the Married Quarters. When I'd answered the knock on the door that Wednesday morning, I'd been surprised to find the soldier delivering the post standing on our doorstep, holding out a white envelope to me. 'Not swimming this morning?'

he asked me. He was a private from Connemara. We had chatted once or twice at the Men's Side.

I shook my head. 'The oul' rain,' I said. 'I hope it stops soon.'

He grinned at me, and the small piece of paper that was covering a shaving cut on his cheek puckered up. I guessed he was about eighteen. 'The holidays aren't much good when it's raining.'

'They're not,' I agreed. I took the letter from him, turning the envelope so that I could read the writing.

'It's for your Mammy,' he said. He spoke with the same accent as Seamus Costello. The rain fell upon him but he made no move to leave our doorstep. At the Men's Side he'd told me that he had five brothers and five sisters: he hadn't seen them since he'd joined the army a few months previously. I wondered what his mother was like.

'I'd better bring the letter in to my mother,' I said.

'Good luck, so,' he said. 'Sure I might see you down at the Men's Side later on.'

'If the oul' rain stops,' I said.

'I have two more to deliver,' he said, holding up two brown envelopes. 'They're upstairs.'

'Good luck, so,' I said.

'Good luck.' He hurried away then, in the softly falling rain. I watched him until he ducked into the Arch.

When I went back into the kitchen, Mammy was still working on the range, although I'd told her there was no need, since it was already shinier than any range in the Married Quarters. She had her sleeves pulled up above her elbows; her face was flushed with effort as she applied the black lead vigorously to the range. 'There's a letter for you, Mammy,' I said to her, 'but I can't make out the postmark, it's blurred.'

'Nosey parker,' my mother said good-humouredly.

'Who is the letter from, Mammy?' Miriam asked. She was putting away the mugs and bowls in the glass case after the breakfast.

'We'll have to open it to find out,' Mammy answered her, 'unless your brother manages to read it through the envelope.'

'Superman could do that with his X-ray vision,' I said. I was going to add that Brother Edmond could probably do it also, but I thought better of it – Mammy didn't approve of what she called 'smart aleck' remarks.

'Can I open the letter, Mammy?' Miriam asked.

My mother looked first at Miriam, then down at her own hands, blackened all over from working on the range. 'Well, I can't open it with hands like these, can I?' she said, holding up her hands. 'You can open the letter,' she added, 'but wait until after I go and wash my hands.' She hurried out of the kitchen. In a moment we heard the tap running in the scullery sink.

'I wonder who it's from,' Miriam said.

'Search me,' I said, 'the postmark is all messed up.'

Miriam examined the envelope very carefully. 'The writing isn't very good,' she said.

'You'd be in trouble in my class for it!'

'And in mine!' Miriam agreed, her eyes widening.

'Right!' my mother said coming back into the kitchen. 'Open the letter, *a ghrá*.'

'In the pictures,' I said, 'they always have a letter-knife to open letters when the maid brings them in on a tray.'

My mother gave me a long look. 'We'll have no maids in this house,' Mammy said, 'but we can certainly use a knife to open a letter.' She opened the drawer in the middle of the glass case and took out one of the army yellow-handled knives. She held the knife out to Mariam, handle first. 'Be careful,' Mammy said to her. Miriam tried to get the top of the knife into the small opening at the side of the envelope. Her mouth pursed in concentration. 'Let me show you,' my mother said. She took the letter and the knife from my sister. She laid the white envelope on the corner of the kitchen table, holding it down with her left palm, and showed Miriam how to edge the knife sideways under the flap of the envelope. She pushed the knife gently to open a small cut in the top of the envelope. 'Now you do it,' she said, handing Miriam the knife. My sister worked at the task with furrowed forehead, worrying the envelope open with short uneven cuts. When she had finished, she looked at Mammy with a little smile of satisfaction. Small curls of paper lay shrivelled on the table beside the opened envelope. 'Good,' said Mammy, 'now you can take the letter out for me.' Miriam withdrew two folded sheets of paper from the envelope. They were lined sheets, covered with large writing on both sides. When Mammy took the letter in her hands you could see her face easing into a smile.

'Who is it from, Mammy?' I asked again.

She answered me without raising her eyes from the letter. 'It's from my mother,' she said, 'from your Granny.'

I knew my mother came from a town about fifty miles away. It might as well have been in another world: the Oregon Trail and the badlands of Dakota seemed closer than that town where Mammy had grown up. Sometimes, late at night, when the smaller children were in bed, she'd talk a little to Miriam and me about Granny up in that town, and the firelight from the range would soften her face into a repose of memories. She hadn't known her father: he'd come home wounded from the war and had died when Mammy was very young. My unknown grandfather's war wounds seemed altogether more remote, less real, than the perils fearlessly faced by Kit Carson in the Wild West of my comics.

'Why is Granny writing to you?' Miriam asked. 'It's not Christmas-time.'

Mammy looked at her but said nothing. We watched as she read the letter again. When she concentrated, you could see the lines deepening in her forehead, like Miriam's when she was doing her homework. Her reading finished, she nodded her head as if silently speaking to herself. She refolded the letter and put it back into its envelope. She turned away then, to reach up to the high mantel-piece, where she placed the letter behind the alarm-clock. When she faced us again, she was smiling. 'I have a surprise for the two of you,' she said.

Miriam and I looked at Mammy, and then at each other. 'What?' we asked together.

'The two of you are going up to your Granny's for your holidays,' Mammy said.

And again Miriam and I looked at each other. Going on holiday – it was surely a mirage, such as parched pioneers imagined they saw in the desert of Nevada! It was Miriam who produced the practical question. 'Will we be going on the bus or train, Mammy?' she asked.

Mammy laughed. 'Indeed you won't!' she exclaimed. 'Sure where would I find the money to pay for two of ye on the bus or on the train!' Mammy saw the puzzlement on both our faces. 'Ye'll have a great trip!' she said gaily. 'Ye'll be going up tomorrow in the bacon factory van!'

The bacon factory van was late.

'He won't forget to come for us, will he, Mammy?' Miriam asked.

The three of us were standing at the chapel gate, outside the Barracks. Behind us, on the ground, was the small brown suitcase containing our clothes and some books and comics.

'Alec won't forget,' Mammy said. 'He probably just got delayed in some shop in town.'

I wasn't fully reassured by her words. The mirage might yet disappear into thin air. 'I'll check on the time,' I said. I dashed into the Gate. 'I'm just checking the time,' I said to the PA. The clock in the Gate said a quarter past two.

'Sure you checked the time only two minutes ago,' Bartley said, lifting and resettling his red-peaked cap on his head. I ignored him. What would Bartley know about going on holiday? What would he care about Alec arriving late in the bacon factory van?

I was panting when I arrived back at the chapel gate. 'It's a quarter past two, Mammy.'

'The last time you looked at the clock,' Mammy said, 'it was twelve minutes after two.'

I couldn't believe that my mother was coming out with the same stuff as Bartley. 'The van was supposed to be here at two o'clock!' I protested.

'Sometimes, Kevin, you have to wait for things to come to you.' There was an edge of amusement in her voice, as if she were teasing me. I liked it when she teased me.

'Tell us again about the driver of the van, Mammy,' Miriam said. 'What's his name?'

'His name is Alec,' Mammy answered. 'We grew up together. We were in the same class at school.' We knew all this. Mammy had told us the night before when she was putting our things into the brown suitcase. I fidgeted from one foot to the other, wondering yet again why girls asked such silly questions.

'Was Alec your boyfriend, Mammy?' Miriam asked.

My mother laughed. 'Is it Alec?' she said. 'Musha, God help your head, child!' Her body shook in laughter at the thought of it.

'Look, Mammy!' Miriam shouted. 'The van! It's coming!'

And it was. The small, cream-coloured van was cruising sedately towards us. Through the windscreen we could barely see Alec, white-shirted, wearing a red, spotted tie, sitting bolt upright with the steering-wheel gripped firmly in his small hands. The van drew to a halt beside us.

When Alec stepped out of the van, I could see why Mammy had been laughing. Alec wasn't even as tall as myself. 'How'r'ya, Sara!' he said, taking my mother's hand in his. 'You're lookin' great, girl!'

'You're lookin' well yourself, Alec!'

For a few moments Miriam and I didn't exist. It was as if these two grown-ups were back at school again. My mother threw names at Alec, names of people I had never heard of, and he threw information back at her, a wedding here, a child born there, somebody had lost a job and someone else was back from England on a visit. My impatience vanished, while I stood there outside the Barracks, picking up these few crumbs of knowledge of my mother's other life, before the Barracks. Finally, their breathless exchange of information seemed to run entirely out of breath. My mother pressed him to come inside Number 2 'for a quick cup in your hand', but Alec was adamant: somebody in town had delayed him and he was already running behind time. He would have to be on the road. His refusal meant there was no need for me to protest. She introduced us to Alec then, and it was strange to be mumbling hello and to be shaking hands with an adult stranger.

'The girleen,' Alec said to my mother, 'is like yourself, Sara, but I don't know who the young fellow is like – is he like the other side? Or has he a look of your own father?'

'Ah, sure, maybe he's like himself, Alec.'

'Anyway, they're grand-lookin' childer,' Alec said, 'and they're a credit to you, Sara.'

'Let ye be off so,' my mother said. It was time to go. Alec opened the back door of the van and there was a glimpse of bacon and rashers as he stored the brown suitcase inside the vehicle. My mother looked at Miriam and myself. 'Give your Mammy a kiss,' she said to us. She bent down and for a moment Miriam clung to her with her arms around Mammy's neck. Miriam's eyes were wet when Mammy released herself. I felt my mother's arms around me and I let her kiss me. I could see Bartley standing outside the Gate, watching us, and I didn't return her kiss. 'Off with ye so,' Mammy said.

Miriam got into the van first. It was cramped, with the two of us sitting on the single passenger seat beside Alec.

'We're off then!' Alec called, waving to my mother, and he eased the van out into the road. We waved to Mammy and she waved back. I twisted on the seat to look back through the rear window of the van. I had a last glimpse of my mother, standing outside the chapel, motionless, with her right hand held up in farewell. It would be two weeks before I saw her again.

'God give me patience with you!' Aunt Dot said. 'Will you for God's sake eat up your dinner!'

'I have enough, I can't eat any more,' Michael said.

'How could you have enough?' You could tell that Aunt Dot was about to explode. 'Sure you've hardly taken a spoonful of your dinner!'

'I told you I don't want any more, Mammy!' My cousin Michael's voice was raised also. 'Why can't you leave me alone? I don't want this rotten oul' dinner!'

'Mind yourself, talking to your mother like that, or it's a good clip on the ear you'll be gettin' for yourself.'

Michael said nothing. He pushed the plate of mashed potatoes and peas and sausages into the middle of the table. He had barely touched the meal.

Aunt Julia came in from the scullery, where she'd been washing her hands. She had to be back at her job in the bacon factory in an hour. 'Don't tell me he's not eatin' his dinner again,' Aunt Julia said.

'God give me patience with him,' Aunt Dot said again.

'Sure why won't you eat up your dinner,' Aunt Julia pleaded with Michael. 'Don't you see the way Kevin and Miriam eat up their dinners?'

I didn't want to catch Michael's eye. I hated it when Aunt Dot and Aunt Julia cited Miriam and me as examples to be followed. If Michael didn't want to eat his dinner, that was fine by me. I just didn't want my aunts dragging me into this debate. It happened every time we sat down to eat in Granny Garvey's house. Any moment now, I thought, they'd start offering Smarties.

'Won't you eat a bit more,' Aunt Julia asked coaxingly, 'if we put a few Smarties in it for you?'

'No!' Aunt Dot snapped. 'He got Smarties in his dinner yesterday – he's not getting them again today.'

It was hard not to smile about having Smarties in your dinner. I had to turn away and look out the window. The sun glinted on the silver handlebars of my two aunts' bicycles, leaning against the window-sill on the footpath outside Granny's house. Neither Aunt Dot nor Aunt Julia would let me ride their bikes. 'You might fall and hurt yourself,' they said, with that adult finality that would entertain no argument.

'Musha, will you leave the boy alone,' Granny Garvey said. 'Sure he knows himself when he has enough.' Granny always stood up for Michael. She'd been quiet up to this, silently eating her own dinner.

'What kind of talk is that, Mother?' Aunt Dot remonstrated. 'How could he have enough when he hasn't eaten anything at all?'

'All the same,' Granny said, 'why don't you just leave the boy alone?'

'Because he has to eat!' Aunt Dot hissed, grabbing the plate of uneaten food from the centre of the table. She dug the spoon into the mashed potato and held the heaped-up spoonful in front of Michael's face. 'Eat!' she commanded.

Across the table Michael caught my eye. You could see the laughter dancing in his blue eyes. I had to look away for fear I might burst out laughing. Michael pursed his mouth firmly shut. He shook his head so vigorously that you'd be afraid it might separate itself from his shoulders.

'Eat!' his mother repeated, more loudly this time.

Michael's eyes opened ever wider, as if the amusement were greater. It was impossible not to like my cousin, even if his eating habits would have been considered bizarre in the Married Quarters.

'Maybe if you tried him with a few oul' Smarties,' Aunt Julia said.

The first time Miriam and I had witnessed the dinner-with-Smarties, we'd been speechless with astonishment. Afterwards, when we were alone, we'd discussed the wonder of a plate of mashed potato, studded with multicoloured Smarties, being spoonfed to our cousin, Michael. I could almost envy him such an exotic fare, yet the very notion of such spoonfeeding was alien to the Barracks. Michael was ten, the same age as myself.

I knew I wouldn't be able to contain the laughter when Michael winked at me. It was a flashing wink, surreptitiously done, when his mother had turned away to say something to Aunt Julia. When Aunt Dot turned back, again brandishing the spoon of potato, Michael's mouth was sealed tight in a deadpan face. I stood up from the table abruptly. 'Where are you going?' Aunt Dot demanded.

'I have to go to the lav,' I sputtered, trying not to laugh.

'Don't talk with your mouth full,' Aunt Julia said.

'And say "excuse me",' Aunt Dot added.

Michael flashed a second wink at me. 'Excuse me,' I gulped into my hand. I dashed from the kitchen, through the scullery and out the back door into the small yard. It was a warm day, and the smell from the shed was worse than usual. There was no indoor lavatory in my grandmother's house: you had to use a bucket in the shed in the backyard. Horseflies hovered in clouds beside the back wall, over the soft ground that was dug and re-dug to bury the lavatory stuff.

I hung around the yard for a while. The big black rooster from the Flanagans', a couple of doors away, strutted on the back wall and crowed against the mid-day sun. He crowed every morning too, at first light. Michael, sleeping beside me in the double bed in the back bedroom, snored on, dead to the cock's crowing. The first morning I'd heard it, I'd slipped out of bed, wearing my father's grey army shirt, and watched through the small window as the pale sun lighted up the field behind the house, and then the river brightened in the brightening light, and the dark stone of the barracks across the river stirred from its own shadows. It wasn't a proper barracks, like the one at home. There were only a few soldiers there now. My grandmother said that Mammy had met my father when he had been stationed there, during the Emergency. I didn't want to ask her to explain what the Emergency was. I'd find out from Mammy when I got home.

In another three days Miriam and I would be travelling home again in the bacon factory van. My two aunts worked in the bacon factory. In the mornings I'd hear them getting ready in the front bedroom, which they shared with Granny. Miriam slept there as well: it was a big room with plenty of space for the four single beds. I'd wait until Aunt Dot and Aunt Julia had left for work before going downstairs for tea and toast. You toasted the bread on a fork that you held over the open fire. There was an iron hook over the fire to hang the kettle on.

My grandmother talked non-stop during breakfast. She talked a lot at other times, too: the words came pouring out of her mouth in a hurrying torrent that seemed always to be trying to overtake itself. She talked often about my mother. At first I didn't know who she meant when she spoke about 'Sareen'. Nobody else used the name 'Sareen' for Mammy. It made me feel that perhaps Mammy had been my grandmother's favourite as a child, perhaps because she'd been the baby. Whenever adults called to the house, or if we met them up the town, Granny always introduced Miriam and me as 'Sareen's childer'.

Coming out of the ice-cream shop with Aunt Julia we'd met a curly-haired woman who said she'd been to school with my mother. After inquiring about Mammy, and how many brothers and sisters we had, the curly-haired woman asked: 'And where do you live?'

'In the Barracks,' I answered. 'We live in the Barracks.'

'Oh.' For a moment the woman was silent. 'Wouldn't you prefer,' she asked then, 'to have a house of your own?' The curly-headed woman didn't seem to understand.

'We have our own house.' I explained patiently. 'Number 2 in the Married Quarters.'

Aunt Julia and the woman smiled at each other. The woman told us to remember her to my mother and she went off smiling, swinging her shopping-bag. I watched her go, still puzzling over her silly question. I thought of her now, looking across the field towards the barracks above the river. Not only did the barracks here not have many soldiers, but it also lacked a Married Quarters. Perhaps the curly-haired woman who had gone to school with Mammy didn't realise that families could also live in a barracks.

Michael came out then. He was my own height and burlier too, but we'd wrestled on the day I arrived and I'd knocked him down. I was glad that he no longer wanted to fight with me. 'Did you eat your dinner?' I asked him.

He laughed, a high-pitched, giggling laugh. 'No,' he said. 'I'll buy a bar of chocolate after my Mam goes back to work.'

'She'll kill you,' I said, 'if she finds out.'

'Sure she never finds out,' Michael said.

It seemed to Miriam and me that Michael always had money. He often bought a sixpenny bar of chocolate, not just the long narrow bar that you could buy for threepence. When Granny gave him money, she'd warn him not to tell his mother; Aunt Julia issued the same warning whenever she pressed money into his hand. The money that Aunt Dot gave him on Fridays, after she was paid at the bacon factory, was official pocket money which had to be concealed from nobody. I knew about regular pocket money from the books I read.

Miriam and I shared in this extravagance of pocket money: whatever amount was given to Michael was given also to us. And on Friday evenings we had shared in the weekly treat at the ice-cream parlour on the corner of the town's main street, when Aunt Dot came home from the bacon factory. In the canteen at home you could buy a tuppenny wafer, cut from the hard block, but here the ice-cream fell whipped and creamy into a stemmed glass dish, and the girl behind the counter decorated it with twirled frills of red strawberry sauce, and you sat at a white table and ate your ice-cream with a long silver spoon, and you felt like somebody in the pictures and you wished that Art and the other lads could see you now . . .

'You'll be going home in three days,' Michael said to me.

'I know.' Our brown suitcase was packed under the bed in the back room.

'You can take some of my comics,' Michael said then. He was looking across the field towards the barracks as if he were talking only to himself. 'I have lots of them.'

I thanked him. 'Can I have some *Hotspurs*?' I asked.

'Take all the *Hotspurs* if you like,' Michael answered, grinning. It was hard to know how my cousin would react to things. Sometimes, as now, you could take everything he had, and he wouldn't care; other times he'd grab the comic you were reading out of your hands and warn you not to touch his stuff again. But I was pleased about the *Hotspurs*: it was a comic that didn't come into any house in the Quarters, and having a good pile of issues meant that I'd be able to follow the serials. And I liked what we called the 'long stories', the stories told in words, without comic-strip pictures, more like a book than a comic. Michael had more comics than anybody I knew. Along with the *Hotspur*, he got the *Knockout* and the *Eagle* every week.

'D'you like going home?' he asked.

149

'I suppose so,' I said. It would be unmanly to admit that I was dying to get back.

'What's it like, having brothers and sisters in the house?' he wanted to know then. He still didn't look at me, busying himself with beating away the buzzing horseflies with his hands while he spoke out of the corner of his mouth.

I thought of our crowded kitchen, my mother feeding the baby and Jacky mucking up my schoolbooks and Miriam tying Danny's laces, and I thought of Michael's house, with three grown-up women dressing him and putting Smarties in his dinner, and I knew where I'd prefer to be. 'It's okay,' I said. Michael said nothing. I felt sorry for him. 'Why don't you come back with us in the bacon factory van?' I said to him. 'There'll be plenty of room and Mammy won't mind!'

He looked at me then. His eyes weren't dancing. 'They wouldn't let me,' he said, gesturing towards the house.

'But they might!' I insisted excitedly. 'I'll ask along with you!'

Michael shook his head. 'They'd never let me,' he said. 'I just know it.'

And in my heart I knew it too. In this house he was forever surrounded by adults and their peculiar constraints. You could tell just by looking at him that he wasn't tough like the lads at the Barracks: he'd never survive a hard winter in a wagon train scavenging for survival on the Oregon Trail.

'Maybe when your Dad comes home,' I ventured, 'maybe he'd let you come to the Barracks for a while.'

Michael grinned at that. 'It wouldn't make any difference,' he laughed. 'They'd probably tell him what to do as well.' Michael's father had been a soldier before he'd gone to England some years previously. He usually came back for a week every year. It was an arrangement I couldn't fathom. How could your father only be at home for a week every year?

'Is he coming home soon?' I asked.

'Next month,' Michael answered.

He turned to face me. 'Will we go down to the river?' he asked.

I gestured nervously towards the house. 'They'll be giving out,' I said, 'like they were the last time we went down there.'

'Arra, don't mind them,' Michael laughed. 'My mother and Julia are gone back to work, and Granny won't see us.'

'If you're sure – '

'C'mon so,' Michael said.

There was no sign of Granny at the back door. We clambered over the wall of loose stones into the field and headed towards the river. The long grass tickled the backs of our knees.

'Guess what,' Michael said.

'What?'

'When I'm big, I'm going to go to England.'

'Is it to be with your father?'

'I don't know,' Michael said, 'but I'm going to England anyway.'

We were down by the river now, in the shadow of the barracks. The current raced on under the bridge, tideless and waveless, and I longed for the whiteheaded breakers at the Men's Side. Granny and my aunts would have a fit if we went swimming here in the river.

'What're you going to do?' Michael asked, stretching out on the bank above the river.

'When?' I could see the raft coming closer, as I cut my way through the waves, my body as jubilant as my mind.

'When you're big,' Michael said. He hauled himself up off the grass, propping himself up on one elbow. 'What're you going to work at when you're grown up?' He was bulky and dark against the sun, his face half-shrouded by the long grasses. Our tomorrows were shadowy also, half-seen through the iron bars of the high Barracks gates and the printed pages of the two books that I borrowed each week from the library in the courthouse in the town.

'I don't know,' I lied. Oh, I knew all right, but it wasn't for saying out loud on this alien bank of an unknown river.

'Will you join the army, maybe?' Michael asked.

Soldiers walked the landscape of my life: his father, my father, my dead grandfather immortalised in the uniform of the Connaught Rangers, staring down from the big photograph that hung on the wall of Granny Garvey's sitting-room. I would march to another drum, a different bugle. 'No,' I said to him, 'I'm not going to be a soldier.'

'And you have no notion at all,' he persisted, 'of what you're going to be?'

My secret wasn't for telling here, in the shadow of the wrong barracks. On a night at home in Number 2, after we were back at school and maybe when the others were gone to bed, I'd get around to telling my mother that, when I was grown-up, I was going to be a writer of books, spinning exciting tales like those of the Hardy Boys and Bomba the Jungle Boy that now filled my imagination. I smiled to myself, lying there in the long grass in the field behind the house where Mammy had grown up. I could see her looking quizzically at me in the kitchen after I'd tell her; I could even hear the question she was going to ask me. 'And will you get paid,' she would say to me with wonder in her voice, 'for making up stories?'

Michael's voice broke in upon my daydream. 'What are you smiling to yourself about?' he asked.

'Nothing at all,' I said, without opening my eyes. 'I was just thinking about going home again.'

TEN

Mrs Folan herself opened the door of Number 1. I peered past her but could see no sign of Art in the kitchen. 'Is Art coming out?' I asked her. You never asked if somebody was in, only if he was coming out.

'PJ!' You kept wanting to tell Mrs Folan that it was years since her son had gone by his childish name: like an Indian boy assuming his proper name when he became a brave, Art could never again be called anything except Art. It could be confusing to be called by two names and anyway Art was now ten and a half – sometimes I resented his being a few months older than me.

From behind Mrs Folan came the sound of the lavatory flushing and then the door opened and Art came out, hitching his braces up to his shoulders. 'Are they down there yet?' he called out, waving to me.

'My father said they were starting at eleven.'

'We better hit the trail so,' Art said.

'Is it the hurlers again?' his mother asked.

'It is, Mam,' Art said, pushing past her behind the door, where they hung the coats. He emerged a moment later with his hurley in his hand.

'I wonder will they do any good this year?' Mrs Folan asked.

Art and I paused on the doorstep, looking at each other in puzzlement. Hurling was man-talk, not squaw-talk. 'Sure they're bound to win on Sunday, Mam,' Art said indulgently.

His mother snorted. 'I'm hearing that every year since I came to the Barracks,' she said indignantly, 'and I haven't seen them win it yet.'

'It'll be different this year, Mam,' Art said seriously. 'If you were down the pitch studying tactics like us, you'd be able to weigh up the pros and cons and make a proper judgment.'

Mrs Folan laughed, a big laugh that was full of the morning sun and the certain knowledge that she was being teased. 'You're full of oul' *seafóid*!' *Seafóid* meant codology: Art's mother came from Aran and she often used Irish words. 'Make sure you weigh up the pros and cons yourself and be here at one o'clock or you'll be studying tactics with nothing for your dinner.' We could hear her laughing to herself after she had closed the door.

Art was grinning to himself, as if amused by the daft antics of a small child who didn't know any better, but inwardly I was worried. 'Maybe your mother is right,' I said to Art.

'Nah! Sure what would women know about hurling!' It was true. Girls tried to play hurling – they called it *camogie* – but they succeeded only in looking foolish.

'All the same,' I said to Art, 'your mother is right – they've never even won a semi-final.'

'Sure what're you talking about? Didn't they win it in 1923!'

'It' was the All-Ireland Hurling Final and we all knew that piece of ancient history. 1923! It might as well be the Stone Age ... thirty years ago ... sure we weren't even born! Since then our county hadn't even won a semi-final in the championship although, by some organisational oddity that was never examined or explained, we were allowed to play each year in the semi-final. Now my father was on the team – had been for as many years as I could remember – and yet another All-Ireland semi-final was less than a week away. Of a sudden it seemed cold, walking in the lee of the Barracks wall, as if Art's mother's words had put to flight the bright sun of a July morning.

'I hope you're right,' I said doubtfully.

'Of course I'm right! I'll bet you a tenner I'm right!'

'A tenner?'

'Forget the tenner! Who cares about a lousy tenner? I'll bet you a hundred quid I'm right!'

'Make it a million!' I shouted.

'Or a billion!' Art cried. He bent and picked up a small stone from the ground. 'He's going through!' Art cried, imitating the voice of Micheál O'Hehir, who was famous among us for his commentaries on the wireless. 'He beats one man! Side-steps another! He's still got the *sliotar* on his hurley! He has only the goalie to beat! He takes a shot! It's in the net!' Art struck the pebble forcefully with his hurley and it ricocheted off the wall of the Barracks. 'It's a goal! The men of the west have scored – and there goes the full-time whistle! The westerners are through to the final!' Art stopped, panting as much from the exertions of his commentary as from his goal-scoring feat. His freckled face was exultant with the moment.

In that moment I knew that we could win on Sunday. 'The westerners are through to the final': it had a ring of glory about it, the way the papers called us 'the men of the west', like the other heroes of another west. 'C'mon!' I shouted, and together we sprinted towards the Gate. The county team was training on the Barracks playing-fields. Where else would they train except at the centre of the universe?

Clouds of steam filled the station. They billowed upwards from the engine and were blown back in upon the platform by the light early-morning breeze. The Apaches and the Commanches could have sent messages across the West all day long if they'd managed to haul a couple of steam-engines to the top of their message-mountains. Mammy and I were sitting opposite each other in the window seats of the compartment. Three men wearing caps were also seated there although they kept to the corridor end of the compartment, leaving a small space on the seats between us. All three of them were smoking: it was hard to tell if there was smoke going out the window or steam coming in.

'It's a powerful day for it,' one of the men said, glancing towards my mother.

'It is to be sure, thank God,' Mammy said.

The man who had spoken looked out the window at the steam-laden platform. 'Powerful altogether,' he said, as if to himself. He was wearing a grey suit and a grey tweed cap.

'It'll suit our lads,' one of his companions said, also peering through the station mists. You couldn't even see the football machine or the printing machine for the steam.

'Down to the ground,' the third one said, 'it'll suit them down to the ground.'

'Sure we hope it will anyhow,' I heard Mammy say.

I said nothing. Mammy would get vexed if I wondered aloud whether our compartment companions thought the match would be played in the middle of a dense cloud and how they could conclude that this would suit 'our fellows' better than the opposition. I thought of telling them that my father had no particular skills in seeing through mists but that too would merit the inevitable frown of dismay from Mammy. I smiled to myself, thinking of what I'd tell Art and the rest of the lads about my day out on the excursion.

When Mammy had told me I'd be going up for a match on the 'excursion' I'd been simultaneously elated and mystified. For once I'd been reluctant to ask Mammy for an explanation: everybody else seemed to know what 'an excursion' was and my ignorance seemed shameful. All through first Mass my attention had wandered, and our walk down the Line seemed never-ending: it had been almost anti-climactic to find the usual green train standing in the station. But exciting too: it was my first-ever journey on a train.

'Won't be long now,' the first fellow said, taking a silver pocket-watch from his waistcoat. His long red face was made even longer by the jowls that hung like flaps under his jaws.

'Any minute now,' the second fellow said, also studying a large watch which seemed small in the palm of his huge hand.

'Any minute at all,' the third fellow said. Alone among the three he wore no waistcoat: I figured that was the reason he had no pocket-watch. He was skinnier than the others too: maybe you had to be fat to have a waistcoat and a pocket-watch.

Above the clanking noise of the train we suddenly heard the piercing blast of the whistle. The clanking noise seemed louder. 'We're off,' the fellow with the jowls said.

On the platform two men rushed past our window, their gaberdines draped across their arms. A door opened and slammed again. The men in our compartment laughed. 'The last of the Mohicans,' the fellow without a waistcoat said, and I looked at him in surprise. He caught me looking at him and winked at me. I blushed.

'Better late than never,' the fellow with the jowls said. He stroked one jowl between his thumb and forefinger as he spoke, and I thought of my father carefully shaving his hard, lean face at the sink in the scullery, and I wondered how this fellow managed to shave that loose, folding flesh without actually slicing it off.

The train gathered speed as we clanked out of the station. Ollie McCormack's cottage came into view, framed in the window of the train. I had never seen the Line like this. I picked my way between the men's legs – Mister Jowls sat in one corner facing his two companions – and stepped out into the corridor. There was a hollow rumble as the train crossed Lough Atalia bridge: the waters of the lake, glinting in the sunlight, slid away behind us like a fading reflection.

I waited until we had crossed the middle bridge before I stepped back inside the compartment. The men were engaged in a demolition of the reputation of the opposition's full-back line: once more I had to thread my way between their outstretched and unmoving shining shoes. 'Paddy Walsh's bridge coming up,' I said to Mammy.

She smiled at me, nodding. She was wearing a blue shop-bought cardigan over a new white blouse that looked even whiter above the wide black elastic belt around her small waist. The soft beret that perched sideways on her dark hair was the colour of our county, a dark maroon.

'It's like being left by yourself on a deserted island,' I'd said to her in the kitchen a few days previously.

'What is?' she'd asked. She'd pulled the tray out of the oven and was concentrating on inserting a knitting-needle into a sultana cake.

'Our colours,' I said. 'Maroon – it's like the same as being dumped alone on an island.'

She'd laughed, pushing the tray back in: the cake needed another little while in the oven. 'Where d'you get your notions? Sure nobody is going to maroon you anywhere.'

She'd been laughing quietly to herself as she wiped the knitting-needle on her apron. That was when she'd told me about going together to the match on the excursion. It had seemed only a dream, another game, as impossible as riding a real stallion in the wide-open spaces of Montana.

What had seemed only a dream was now made real. I stood at the window, watching the Furze rush past as the train gathered speed. Beyond the Furze lay the sweep of the bay: in the white lighthouse the lighthouse-keeper would be listening later in the day to the wireless commentary on the match.

I forgot about the lighthouse and its keeper as we steamed onwards. I could see the plateau rushing towards us, the green doors of the Barracks garages for the army lorries, closed now for

Sunday, and, behind the garages, the grey walls of the Barracks itself.

Art and Tommy and Bobby were standing on top of the embankment. I could see their heads turning this way and that, scanning the train for me. I waved frantically, calling out, 'Here! Here!'

They couldn't hear me, but they spotted me as we flashed past: I saw Bobby point at me, grabbing Tommy by the sleeve. In a second they were gone, a blur of open mouths and waving hands. The darkness of the Barracks bridge swallowed us up for a second, and then the sunlight came again. I was breathless when I turned from the window.

The three men were watching me with obvious amusement. 'D'you know those lads that were wavin'?'

'Of course I do! Sure don't we all live in the Barracks!' I answered Mister Jowls.

He looked at his two pals, then back at me. 'Ye'll know our corner-back so – Jimmy Brophy?'

I looked at Mammy before answering. 'He's my father,' I said.

Mister Jowls said: 'Well, I declare to God!'

The second fellow said: 'Well, honest to God!'

The third fellow said: 'Honest to God indeed!' Their exclamations seemed to keep time with the rhythm of the train. I wished they would close their mouths: their teeth were yellowed like a Gold Flake packet.

Mister Jowls was their spokesman. He cleared his throat self-consciously. 'Would you be *Missus* Brophy?' he asked.

My mother looked at him. I noticed how she straightened herself in the seat before she answered. 'I am,' she said.

Mister Jowls stood up. His large body seemed to fill the compartment. He took his cap off with his left hand and stretched out his right to my mother. 'I'm fierce pleased to meet you, ma'am. I'm Thomas Brennan and these – ' he turned to the other men, who were now also on their feet ' – these are my brothers, Ambrose and James.' My mother and Thomas Brennan shook hands, and then the other two men also shook her hand.

The train swayed as we rounded a curve, and the men bumped into each other and reached for the overhead rack to keep their balance. They laughed loudly as they collided, crowding the small floor of the compartment.

158

'What's the *gasur's* name?' Mister Jowls asked. My mother told them, and I felt my hand swallowed up in turn by three huge hard hands. 'Is it your first time goin' up to Croke Park?' Mister Jowls wanted to know.

I nodded.

'Maybe you'll bring them luck,' one of the brothers said.

'We'll need it,' the third brother said.

'You always need a bit of luck to beat Kilkenny,' Mister Jowls said.

The train seemed to accelerate suddenly. The whistle of the train pierced the morning air, three long blasts that blazed across the sky like exultant war-cries.

'Up Skehana!' the three Brennan brothers shouted together as the whistle sounded. They laughed again, and then looked sheepishly at my mother like small children caught messing in High Babies. My mother joined in the laughter. I thought of asking where or what Skehana was, but I decided it didn't matter. What mattered was being there, sharing the laughter of the moment on the way to Croke Park and a semi-final showdown between the men of the west and the Kilkenny cats.

Croke Park was a cauldron of noise, a sea of colour. The green pitch remained green, although you'd expect it to be submerged beneath the waves of noise that rose and broke upon it unceasingly. These waves had a physical force that swept you forward, in response to some passage of play in the field, hurling you down-wards along the steps of terracing, palms outward as if they could create a barrier to lean against. There was no barrier, just another jacket or gaberdine or pullover in front of you, its owner tilted like yourself, striving for balance.

The Brennan brothers gave us sanctuary. Time and again as the waves of people ebbed and flowed and drowning seemed imminent in the maelstrom of waving hands and raucous voices, time and again my mother and I were handed back to safety on the terrace-step that was our personal pontoon, planted with the flag of Thomas Brennan's own shopping-bag of sandwiches and a cake wrapped in greaseproof paper. It was our private capstan, that green and black plaid bag, its mouth gaping to reveal the now-empty flask and carefully folded rectangles of greaseproof paper. James or Ambrose handed you back up to Thomas, and you planted your feet gratefully on your very own piece of territory and braced yourself for the next swell.

Whatever drama was unfolding on the pitch below us was incomprehensible to me. Our team wore maroon jerseys, with white cuffs and collars; Kilkenny wore shirts such as I had never seen before, narrow vertical stripes of black and amber, that made the players seem like dangerous wasps at large in the September afternoon. They seemed to be buzzing everywhere, chasing from end to end, hurrying from touchline to touchline. They hunted in swarms, striking our hapless maroon-clad heroes with Apache-like menace, forever outgunning us.

Incredibly, as the match entered its final moments, our heroes of the west were leading by a solitary point. The din rose on the terraces, the waves unleashed themselves again as the angry wasps (why did they call them cats?) came buzzing again around our goalmouth.

Thomas Brennan turned to Mammy and me, eyes flashing and jowls flapping. 'We're going to do it!' he roared. 'We're going to do it!'

James half-turned in the crush, waving his watch by its silver chain. 'Still a couple of minutes left!' You could see the tension jostling with the hope in his red face.

On the pitch the players swarmed around our goal. It didn't matter that I was unable to follow the play: it was enough to know that we led by a point and that time was running out. I could see my father in the corner, the big Number 4 on the back of his shirt, shadowing the Kilkenny Number 13. They moved together like dancers, sidestepping, feinting and darting like Siamese twins who could hear their own private music in their heads.

My father had grown up in Kilkenny, had been in the same class at school as the Kilkenny fellow in the Number 13 jersey. Now they were on opposite sides, like Billy the Kid and Pat Garrett, in their private duel. Or like Cuchulainn and Ferdia: Brother Edmond had told us the tale, how they had learned together as young men the noble arts of the warrior and how, years later, in single combat, Cuchulainn, the hero of Ulster, had slain the friend of his youth. I wondered if they spoke to each other down there on the pitch, my father and his old school-pal, as they tussled for victory in the dying moments of this struggle.

The referee blew his whistle. A split second of silence fell upon the crowd, and then a single roar erupted from thousands of hoarse throats. The air was full of waving caps coloured black and amber.

'What happened, Mammy?' I struggled to make myself heard amid the crescendo. 'Did Kilkenny win?'

'It's a free for Kilkenny, right in front of the posts.'

It was Thomas Brennan who answered me. His face was solemn; his jowls hung lower, like the flag at half-mast over the Barracks when a soldier died.

The referee was directing operations in front of our goal. A handful of our fellows, my father among them, lined up to face the free puck. The Kilkenny Number 13 was standing beside the *sliotar*.

'He's deadly with these,' someone said behind me.

'Sure he couldn't miss,' said someone else.

I felt my mother take my hand in hers. Her face was white when I looked up at her.

'He might go for the goal,' Ambrose said.

'Devil a chance,' James answered. 'He'll take his point.'

'And they'll win the replay, God blast it!' There was anger and frustration in Thomas Brennan's voice.

A hush fell upon the entire stadium as Jim Langton, my father's old school-friend, bent over the ball. He flexed his hurley against the sod, moulding the stick, shaping it, like an extension of his wrist.

The *sliotar* was raised on his hurley.

In the silence I could hear Mammy whispering a Hail Mary.

Langton struck the ball towards our citadel.

The *sliotar* didn't rise high enough to clear the crossbar. A defender's hurley got the ball, batted it out of the goalmouth.

Pandemonium broke loose on the terraces. The shouts of triumph were ours now. The fort was held, the Indians repulsed. There were caps in the air again, but they were maroon and white now: the black and amber banners were trailing in the dust.

The referee blew his whistle. It was all over. The day was ours. Against all odds the westerners had won a great victory. I didn't mind my mother kissing me in front of so many people: nobody noticed anyway. I noticed the film of tears in her eyes.

Thomas Brennan ceremoniously shook hands with his brothers, and then with Mammy and myself.

'I've travelled a long way and waited a long time to see this day!' he said, and his voice squeaked, like a girl's, after all the shouting. His eyes were wet too. Grown-ups were like that, always expecting the worst, and then crying when they landed the prize.

'Next stop the final!' Ambrose Brennan roared hoarsely. We were surrounded by our own: a great shout rose up, the clamour of an exultant tribe, masters of the field.

There were crowds on the pitch too, swamping the players, and I couldn't see my father. I hoped that he was shaking hands with his old school-pal. Victorious warriors were always magnanimous.

Through the final weeks of August our county team trained on the army pitch, in the shadow of the grey barracks. All day, every day, breaking only for Saturday and Sunday, the hurlers performed their simple rituals. They played games of backs-and-forwards among themselves, playing into the goal closest to the army garages. They went for long, slow runs around the edge of the pitch, shouting at each other as they wound their way along the touchline. They ran two by two in fiercely competitive sprints for twenty and thirty yards. They leap-frogged their way down the pitch and back up again. They rehearsed taking frees and defending against them. When they stopped to talk to you they smelled of sweat. They chatted often to us. We fetched the *sliotar* for them from behind the goals. Sometimes, when the ball was pucked over the sideline and down the slope into the beds of tall ferns that bordered the Furze, we searched long and diligently, not always with success. They signed their names in our autograph books, and we compared their inscriptions and their signatures. There was general agreement among us that the laziest autographer was the fellow who looked to see if the inside back-cover of your book was empty, so that he might write above his name, 'By hook or by crook I'll be the last in your book'. The inside back-cover of a fellow's autograph book was always one of the first pages to be filled.

We forgave the members of the team their lack of originality in the matter of signing autographs. They were shaping up well, we told one another sagely, clustered in a knot behind the goal. They were fitter and faster to the ball, their stick-work more skilful. No matter what the newspapers said, they were good enough to beat Cork and win the All-Ireland.

'They're good enough to take the trophy,' I announced solemnly as we watched the last training session, just days before the final. I used the word 'trophy' with deliberate relish: it was a good word, rhyming with 'Brophy'. None of the lads from the Quarters ventured to disagree with my assessment: my status as a commentator was assured, not just because my father was on the team but also because I was the only one among us who had been to Croke Park. And Mammy had told me that I'd be going up for the final too. The rest of them would have to make do with Micheál O'Hehir on the wireless.

'The trophy will be coming west on Sunday night, pardner,' Art said.

'The West's Awake!' Tommy said, quoting the title of a song we had been taught by Brother Edmond.

'The West's Awake!' we all chorused together.

The newspapers didn't think so. Cork were certain to win, they said. Cork had a not-so-secret weapon called Christy Ring: he was the greatest hurler since Cuchulainn, they said, a claim which was rewarded with whoops of derision inside the Barracks. What couldn't be denied, however, was that Christy Ring had won more All-Ireland medals than any other hurler.

And our team was too old, the papers said. When they said this, they singled out my father, and Seanie Duggan, recognised by every follower who knew anything about the game as the greatest goalie that ever lived, and the forwards, Inky Flaherty and Josie Gallagher, and sure didn't everybody know that these men could score points from every angle of the pitch, with their eyes closed? The newspapers said that my father and the others were 'past their prime' at thirty-three. We scoffed: they were all old, as far as we were concerned, whether they were twenty-three or thirty-three. 'Swan Song For Veterans', one paper said. We laughed over that – swans with hurleys in their beaks, singing songs as they flew above the Barracks. And anyway, wasn't Christy Ring bald – couldn't you see that clearly in the pictures in the newspapers! It just went to show, we agreed, that newspapers hadn't a clue. The All-Ireland hurling trophy, we reassured ourselves fiercely, was ours, no matter what the papers said, for the first time since 1923.

It wasn't quite so easy to reassure ourselves about the curse on the team. It was because of the curse upon the county's hurling team that we had never been able to repeat our sole victory in the All-Ireland. It was Tommy who told us the story. You had to give credence to Tommy in such matters: his father, the Barracks barber, had won an All-Ireland football medal with the county ages and ages ago, before any of us were even born.

Our hurling team had been cursed from the altar by a priest. Nobody knew exactly where, or when. The team had stopped off to hear Mass on their journey to play a match. They had crowded together at the back of the church, impatient to be on their way to the venue. They were late, that was the trouble, and the priest was going on forever. When it came to reciting the Hail, Holy Queen and the three Hail Mary's at the end of Mass, the players' impatience got the better of them: as one they rose from their benches in the back of the church and began to shuffle their way noisily to the door. The priest, disturbed by the commotion, broke off his recitation of the Hail Mary and rose from his knees. He called the players back to complete their prayers but they were heedless. 'I curse ye and all the teams that come out of your county after ye!' the priest intoned. 'I curse ye for this insult to God in His own house – ye'll never have another day's luck and ye'll never win another All-Ireland!'

We fell silent when Tommy finished his tale. We could see the priest standing there on the altar, uniformed in his vestments, his face red with indignation, his hand outstretched as he cursed our hurlers for generations to come. The story of the curse was taboo. You could debate the inadequacies of newspaper writers but what could you do about the curse of God?

We lost the final. Maybe it was just that Cork were too good. Our supporters said it was because Christy Ring struck our captain a foul blow with his hurley, so that the captain had to leave the field to have a dozen stitches sewn into his jaw. In my heart I knew that the curse had sealed our fate. Those impious hurlers of long ago had made it impossible for us to win another All-Ireland: how I railed inwardly against them, how I wished they had remained in that unknown church to recite their prayers!

We missed the train home after the match, and Mammy and I trudged disconsolately through the streets of Dublin back to the hotel where my father and the other players were having their dinner after the game. They brought us food, but it was sawdust in our mouths. Somebody located the driver of a bus heading west that night and Mammy and I were given a seat at the back of the crowded vehicle. It was a lonesome journey through the darkness. The passengers drank bottles of stout and the empty bottles rolled along the floor beneath the seats. They broke into song sometimes, but their songs were sad: *The West's Awake* sounded like a lament. We stopped in a small village and the bus emptied into a pub. I told Mammy that I didn't want to go in, that I'd be okay. I sat in the empty bus and let the silence settle upon me. I cleared the steamed-up window with my sleeve and looked at the stars, but they held no answers either.

The bus filled up again. The singing was louder and more frantic, as if the raised voices could hurl back the misfortunes of the day. There were more empties rolling about on the floor of the bus. I let my mother hold my hand.

We were driving through a darkened town when somebody shouted to the driver to stop, that he'd burst if we didn't stop right away. We crossed a long bridge and turned right. The driver brought the bus to a stop in the shadow of a high grey wall.

'C'mon,' Mammy said, 'a breath of air will do us good.' We filed off the bus with the others. In the clear air I could hear the sound of a rushing river.

'Where are we?' I asked Mammy.

'Athlone.'

Athlone was the dead centre of Ireland. It marked the spot on the wireless where you got Radio Eireann. I was too tired to ask Mammy why it said Athlone, when everybody knew that Micheál O'Hehir did his commentary on the matches from Dublin.

'That must be the Shannon,' I said. Mammy nodded. She looked weary, standing in the light from the bus. 'Will we take a look, Mammy?'

She took my hand and we crossed the road together. The noise of the river grew louder. The Shannon was the longest river in Ireland; it was even longer than any river they had in England. The river was a rushing bed of darkness. The whole town was in darkness. We had lost the final but still the whole country seemed to have gone to sleep, as if nothing had happened. Only our bus-load was awake, making its painful way home.

'That's the barracks,' Mammy said, pointing back across the road, 'Custume Barracks.'

You could make out the bulk of the barracks in the darkness. I knew the story of Sergeant Custume, how he and his men had died demolishing the bridge across the river, preventing the advance of King William's army. It pleased me, this naming of a barracks for a sergeant: they were always raising monuments and statues to generals and officers.

'We better go back,' Mammy said.

We turned from the river to cross the road. You had to get on the bus and you had to carry on through the darkness. What was lost was lost: the result of the game could never be changed. Even the two men urinating noisily in the shadows against the wall of Custume Barracks knew that.

ELEVEN

My mother's brother was dying in the san out on the Dublin Road. Uncle Tim was the only brother she had.

She moved about our kitchen and scullery as if in a trance – from the range to the table, table to press, press to sink, like someone we didn't know. And she didn't seem to know us. When she placed the steaming bowls of porridge on the table on the dark mornings of Uncle Tim's last December, the kitchen was warmed by the fire in the range, and your belly was warmed by the hot porridge, but the day was cold without her smile.

On a damp evening after school, with Christmas no more than a week away, I met her at the top of the Line and knew at once that she was returning from the hospital.

'Did you see Uncle Tim, Mammy?' Every day for weeks now she'd been going out to the san after dinner: she'd be rushing the washing-up before we had left the kitchen to go back to school so that she could spend longer with Uncle Tim.

She stopped at the head of the Line and rested her two shopping-bags on the tarred surface of the road. She flexed her ungloved fingers to restore their circulation. I picked up the two bags. They weren't heavy: Mammy did her 'big shopping' in town – what she bought in the shop out the road was mainly items that ran out unexpectedly or, sometimes, shop bread. For a while now Mammy hadn't been baking the daily cakes in the oven of the range.

'Did you see him?' I asked again. Still she didn't answer, but went on flexing her fingers and rubbing them together. Her pale face, framed in the dark folds of her scarf, seemed paler in the early-evening light of the lamp in the chapel garden. I touched her sleeve. 'Is Uncle Tim not getting better?'

She came back to me then. She shivered a moment, her slight body trembling in the chill, and her gaze swept round, as if she were seeing anew the stone chapel, and the grey barracks, and the lighted gate, and, behind me, the Line threading its way above the Furze towards the town. And, finally, her eyes came to rest upon me. 'I don't know if he's able to get better,' she said, 'it's all in God's hands now.'

I touched her sleeve again. I had to ask her. 'Is Uncle Tim going to die?'

She smiled, the kind of wistful smile you got sometimes when she shook her head in dismay at some wrong thing you had said or done. 'It's in God's hands now,' she said again.

'Will we go into the chapel and say a prayer for him?' I asked.

'I don't think I've any prayers left in me,' Mammy said. 'Maybe you'll come out again by yourself later on and say a prayer for him.'

'I will,' I promised her.

We moved slowly towards the Gate, and I could think of nothing to take away the sadness that gripped her. Later, before the PA locked the chapel for the night, I would do as I had promised, and kneel before the blue and white statue of the Blessed Virgin in the top corner of the church, and beg Mary to ask Jesus to make Uncle Tim well and lift the cloak of grief from Mammy's shoulders. Hadn't he brought Lazarus back from the dead? Wouldn't it be just a small miracle to make Uncle Tim well again?

The new PA opened the Gate for us. He was a newcomer to the Barracks: he didn't know the names of all the lads in the Quarters. 'Good-evening, Mrs Brophy,' the new PA said, and I looked at him with kinder eyes, pleased that he knew my mother's name.

Mammy said hello as the PA held the heavy door of the Gate open for us.

'Is there any word on your brother, ma'am?' the PA asked. He was a big fellow with a round face. Even within the confines of the Gate he was wearing the slate-grey raincoat of the PAs against the damp cold of the December evening: the dark mahogany leather of his holster gleamed against the dull grey stuff of the coat.

'There's no change,' Mammy said.

'At least that's not bad news,' the PA said, 'and you can hope for better news tomorrow.'

'Please God,' Mammy said.

'Goodnight so,' the new PA said.

It was strange to be saying goodnight and it wasn't even half past four yet. But you'd think it was later: you had to peer intently to make out the green, white and gold flag hanging listlessly from the pole on top of the Magazine. It was the brightness of the town that had delayed me after school: I'd dawdled alone along Shop Street, after Art and the other lads had gone home, reluctant to leave the Christmas display of books in O'Gorman's window and head for a kitchen that had become a lonely place.

And it was weird to think of Uncle Tim dying: I could only picture him as he had been in the summer, striding from his own house at one end of the street to Granny's at the other end. Everybody knew him, everybody spoke to him. He'd won a scholarship at school, and wore a dark suit with an array of pens in his breast pocket to go to his job in the office at the bacon factory. Sometimes he was accompanied on his walk by his elderly greyhound, Mutt; the dog had won races in his youth but he seemed to spend most of his old age asleep on the footpath outside Uncle Tim's house. The old greyhound seemed to stir only for Uncle Tim. Granny used to complain loudly about the presence in her house of that old flea-bitten hound, but Uncle Tim just laughed his good-natured laugh at her and Mutt snorted, and sometimes farted, on the floor of Granny's kitchen.

'Mutt will be lonesome,' I said aloud. We were walking in the shadow of the Barracks wall towards the Quarters. There was nobody out playing: the whole place seemed deserted.

'I know,' Mammy said.

I wanted to ask her if Uncle Tim's wife might allow Mutt into the house, or if the dog might be admitted into Granny's house, now that Uncle Tim was so sick in the san, but I heard weariness in her voice, and I said nothing. We went together down the steps to the Married Quarters in silence.

I recognised Art's coded rat-tat-tat on the window of Number 2 shortly after tea.

The kitchen was quiet. Mammy had already left, with my father, for her second visit of the day to the sanatorium. Miriam was seated across the table from me, bent over her Irish book: her lips mouthed the words silently as she read. Beside her sat Jacky, mouth pursed and eyes narrowed as he went on sharpening his pencil point: he broke more pencil points than anybody in the whole world – sometimes it seemed that my brother thought pencils existed only to be sharpened, that their use for writing was entirely arbitrary. I watched the pile of pencil shavings on the edge of the table with dismay: in a minute, I had no doubt, Jacky would spray the shavings all over the linoleum floor that Miriam had just swept. Or he'd manage to scatter the wood-flakes across the page on which Danny was laboriously creating with a red crayon stick a misconceived figure of a horse that had five legs (one presumably a tail) and a neck that approximated to a sideways sweeping-brush. When that happened, the peace of our kitchen would undoubtedly be shattered: it was even possible that the baby, now sleeping in the bedroom, would be roused by the replay of the Battle of the Little Big Horn. Best be going, I thought, zipping up my lumber jacket.

There was a louder, longer rat-tat-tat on the window – our secret code for confirmation of the earlier signal. I could imagine Art crouched under the window in the shadows, waiting for my response to his signal.

'That's Art,' Miriam said, without looking up from her book. 'Isn't that your secret code or something?'

'If it's a secret,' I snapped, 'then I can't discuss it, can I?'

She looked up briefly and smiled. 'Tell Art,' she said, stooping again over her Irish book, 'to tell Mary that I can't go out tonight because I'm minding the house.'

'If it *is* Art,' I said with slow deliberation, 'I'll tell him, but it might not be him – it could be anybody tapping at the window.'

Miriam waved her hand in my direction without taking her eyes from the page. 'Okay,' she said, and the nascent laughter in her voice reminded me of Mammy, 'if it *is* Art, tell him.' I turned away. Secret codes should not be discussed with girls, not even a pretty good one like Miriam.

I was closing the kitchen door and crossing the front scullery into the hall, when I heard Danny's shriek of outrage, followed immediately by Jacky's loud protest of indignation, that whatever had happened was 'your own fault!'. Miriam's soothing voice was suddenly drowned by the unearthly crying of the baby.

It was a relief to step out into the darkness and hear Art's whisper from the shadows: 'Sounds like an Indian uprising, pardner.'

'Kids,' I said. 'They're never quiet.'

'They're a bloody nuisance, pardner,' Art said. We sometimes used swear-words, now that we were growing up, especially when our mothers weren't around. 'All set for the expedition?'

I nodded to Art.

'Let's go,' he said. 'Bobby and Tommy will be waiting at the wash-house.'

We'd invited Paul on the expedition too, but his mother wouldn't let him out: it was tough, we all agreed, having no brothers or sisters, despite their nuisance-qualities. Anyway PAs were weird as fathers: the only other PA who lived in the Quarters, apart from John's father, was Harry O'Connell, and the O'Connells had no boys at all in their family, just two girls.

Together Art and I headed around the block of the Married Quarters to rendezvous with our pardners at the wash-house.

The wash-house was a two-story building located behind the Quarters. It was built right up against the back wall of the Barracks, its slated roof rising even higher than the perimeter wall. It was a small structure, having only a single room downstairs and a flight of wooden steps that led to another single room upstairs. When you stood on the upper floor you looked out over the turfyard beyond the Barracks wall and, beyond it, the steel ribbon of the railway line, the curve of the bay and the roof of the tiny school that the Tynans had broken into.

Art and I let ourselves silently into the wash-house. There was no bulb inside, but we could make out the wooden staircase by the light of the standard lamps outside. The sound of shuffling feet upstairs sounded loud in the small place.

'Halt! Who goes there?' Tommy's loud whisper came from the top of the stairs.

'Friends!' Art's whisper was equally loud.

Tommy and Bobby were silhouetted against the moonlight at the top of the stairway. 'Pass, friends.'

We had never progressed beyond this stage of sentry-dialogue: our comics never did either. We'd gone through a spell of watching the sentry on duty opposite the Gate, marching up and down inside his walled-in beat but no matter how long we listened and watched, none of us had ever heard a proper exchange between sentry and approaching stranger. This inevitably cast doubts on the authenticity of sentinel behaviour inside our own Barracks.

We climbed to the top of the stairs. Up here it was brighter than on the ground floor: on one side the great reeks of turf shone like enormous beetles; on the other side, the lines of washing that hung along the rear of the Married Quarters seemed close enough to reach out and touch. (You would do so at your peril: high speed chasing games which often involved galloping full tilt through lines of towels and army shirts drew an immediate rebuke from some open lavatory window – you'd swear the women were crouched within, kneeling beside the lavatory on the stone floor, just waiting for you to go charging through the washing so that they could throw up the small window of the lav and threaten you with the greatest clip on the ear that you ever got.)

We whispered to one another, standing in a huddle at the top of the stairs.

'Everybody all set?' Art asked. Our heads bobbed in agreement.

Bobby cleared his throat. 'The window is open,' he said in a whisper. 'I checked it a few minutes ago.'

'We'll need a look-out,' I ventured.

'I'll do it,' Bobby offered. 'I'll wait at the top of the Arch – if anybody sees me, they'll think I'm waiting for Paul.'

'We need a password,' Art said.

'Sarsfield,' I said quickly.

Art was nodding his head in approval. 'Like at Ballyneety,' he said. 'Sarsfield is the word – '

' – and Sarsfield is the man,' Tommy finished.

It was the best story in our school history-book: Sarsfield, learning that his own name was the English password, had attacked the English wagon-train and blown its deadly cargo of gunpowder sky-high, answering the English sentry who challenged him with the stirring cry: 'Sarsfield is the word and Sarsfield is the man!' For once our history book pages blew the stench of gunpowder into our grateful nostrils.

'Let's go,' Art said. 'We'll meet up at the top of the Arch.'

We'd already hatched our plan. To minimise attention, we would approach in pairs, two from either end of the Married Quarters. Tommy and Bobby would circle the Quarters from the Number 1 end; Art and I would take the passage around the lower end, where the PA who had only daughters lived. The perils of our night-time mission ranged from attacks by renegade redskins to challenges from sonless PAs; there was also the ever-present risk of your mother spotting you in the middle of your mission and calling you in for bed. It was to counteract this last risk that we had devised routes for the expedition which did not take us past our own front doors. Bobby stood the greatest peril: we had to pass through the Arch to get up to the veranda and the target of our mission.

We filed out of the wash-house without speaking. With a backward wave, Tommy and Bobby took off to the right, where they would round the Quarters in front of Art's house. Art and I skirted the wired-in compound which housed the maintenance materials and equipment used by the workman who serviced the Barracks. In the yellow light of the moon the iron barbs of the bullwire fencing gleamed like Apache arrow-heads. We called the compound the Wires.

We passed the O'Connells', where the PA lived with his wife and two daughters: the girls rode bicycles down the Line to their jobs in town. A house of squaws, like Mammy's old house, and Aunt Dot and Aunt Julia cycling to work in the bacon factory. I banished from my mind the death-white face of my Uncle Tim, lying in the ward which was out of bounds to children, and pressed on with Art towards our destination.

Nobody hailed us as we moved on towards the Arch. The December night was cold: curtains were drawn inside the closed windows of the Quarters, and hall doors were shut against the chill. Bobby's mother was not standing sentinel, arms crossed, on the front step of the Arch.

Tommy and Bobby were waiting for us in the middle of the veranda, on top of the Arch. Here was the true centre of the Barracks. We stood in silence listening for intruders or eavesdroppers, but you could only hear the silence of the Barracks, like waves of whispering in a sleeping household. Bobby waved us forward and Art, Tommy and myself huddled closer together, almost bent over one another for mutual protection as the target of our expedition came into view.

That target was the Suttons' Quarters. The Suttons had moved out two days earlier and as yet no new family had moved in. Private Sutton was a small man who drove one of the big army trucks. He seemed to like largeness: his skinny wife towered over him; even his two sons, younger than ourselves, rose above him.

The window of the Quarters was raised slightly: Art and myself managed to squeeze our fingers into the tiny gap. 'Ready?' I whispered.

Art nodded. Together we pushed upwards with our fingertips. The window flew upwards with an ease that startled us. We held our breaths for a moment, staring into the empty kitchen of the Suttons' old Quarters. No sentry challenged us in the darkened Barracks.

'Quickly!' Art hissed. He clambered onto the bluestone window-sill: when he dropped down you'd think the whole Barracks would hear the clump of his boots on the lino. I followed him inside; within seconds we were joined by Tommy. I reached up to pull the window down. I could just make out Bobby standing in the corner of the enlarged area that marked the centre of the veranda. He waved surreptitiously to me as I lowered the window.

The emptiness of the house was overwhelming. The light spilling through the uncurtained windows bathed us in a paleness that was ghostly; I sensed, looking at Art and Tommy, that they too were feeling the unease I felt. The house was spooky: when you moved, you felt a presence at your elbow, as if the Suttons were crouched in the corners of the kitchen, watching you invading their Quarters.

'Let's search for clues,' Art said.

'I need to go,' Tommy said.

We all had to go. We crowded together and urinated loudly and ritually into the white lavatory bowl. Even in the faint light you could see the yellow pee steaming like suds in the lav. When we had finished the silence was frightening again. We backed out of the lav without pulling the chain.

'There might be something in the bedroom,' I whispered.

The latch made a loud clacking noise when I pressed it down to open the bedroom door. The bedroom yielded no clues, nothing that might explain why an apparently sane family would suddenly up stakes and leave the Barracks to go to Coventry. We'd looked it up in the Atlas: Coventry was in the middle of England. Why would anybody want to move there?

Our eyes scanned the empty bedroom. When Kit Carson examined the burnt-out remains of a settler's ranch in the Wild West, he always managed to discover important clues that would identify the marauding Indians – an arrow-flight here, a feather there, a dying man's message scrawled in blood on the fly-leaf of an ancient bible. There were no clues in the Suttons' bedroom to explain their flight: nothing but silence echoing and dust dancing.

'Look!' Art bent towards a piece of cloth in the corner beneath the window. When he held it up you could see that it was one of the hideous knicker-trousers that Mrs Sutton knitted for her boys – they looked like Donald Duck in them, with the tight multicoloured garments stuck to their bottoms.

'I wonder if she'll make them wear them in Coventry,' Tommy mused.

Neither Art nor I answered. The Sutton boys were too young to be in our gang; we had teased them often enough about their unfortunate pants. But we had defended them also, more than once, when they had been made the butt of jokes by civvies in the schoolyard, or on the streets of the town on the way home after school. What would become of them in a place called Coventry, in the middle of England?

'Let's get out of here,' Art said suddenly.

I shivered. The empty house was freezing; the silence was eerie. Art dropped the knitted trousers on the floor as if they were an omen of misfortune.

Nobody spoke as we climbed out through the window of the empty Quarters. Bobby hopped from foot to foot in the shivering cold as he questioned us about what we had found. We were curt with him, although we could not have said why.

Bothered by fears and shames that were both faceless and nameless, we bade one another goodnight and hurried away to our separate Quarters.

Miriam had the red Christmas candle ready; she'd garlanded the jam-jar in which the candle stood with a fringed frock of green crêpe paper. We stood in a semi-circle around the end of the table, waiting for Mammy to lead us in the annual ritual. The curtains were not drawn across the high windows: when you looked out you could see, in the yellow light from the swan-necked lamp that craned from the corner of the Magazine, the steel slab of the armourer's shop door, closed now, like most doors in the Barracks, for the Christmas holidays.

The doors of the Quarters would, as always, remain unlocked on this night when Joseph and Mary would be trawling the streets for sanctuary.

'Can I light the candle now, Mammy?' my sister Martha asked, rattling the box of matches. She was five or nearly five: it often seemed pointless keeping up with precise ages of small children – six months here or there seemed to add not an iota to their store of wisdom. 'Can I light the candle *now*?' Martha demanded again.

My mother looked at her as if surprised by the question. She was still wearing her overcoat. Martha and Danny had waylaid her as soon as she'd come in from her visit to Uncle Tim in the hospital. 'What is it, *a ghrá*?' she asked.

'The candle, Mammy!' There was exasperation in Martha's voice. 'Can I light it?'

I couldn't bear to watch the exaggerated care with which Martha set about opening the box of matches: the tedious antics of small children were sometimes best borne by ignoring them. Instead I watched my mother. She seemed not to be with us. The habitual lines in her forehead seemed to cut more deeply into her pale skin.

It took three strikes before Martha got the match to light. Like all girls she insisted on striking the match *away* from her. Miriam guided Martha's hand and held it steady until the white wick caught flame. For a few minutes we were caught up, even the smaller ones, in a spell of silence. It was a liturgy that never failed to enchant, this lighting of our candle on the kitchen table on the night of Christmas Eve.

Without a word I crossed the kitchen to the door and switched off the light.

'Will we bless ourselves now, Mammy?' Miriam asked.

'Let ye do that,' my mother told us. It was strange, I thought, that Mammy had to be reminded of that. Blessing yourself was an integral part of the ritual.

'Was Uncle Tim better today?' Miriam's voice was hesitant as she asked the question.

'There was no change in him,' Mammy answered. In the candle-light her face was tired. She hardly looked at us. She turned from us, towards the window, although I knew she wasn't seeing the Magazine or the armourer's shop either. 'No change at all in him,' she said, turning back to us.

'Will you be going out to the hospital tomorrow, Mammy?' I asked her.

'I'll have to,' she said.

'But tomorrow is Christmas Day!' I protested.

'Yes!' the others chimed in. 'You can't go to the hospital on Christmas Day!'

She waited for the noise to stop, not looking at us, just staring out the window. Did she see more in the darkness than I could see? Our communal outburst subsided into sullen silence. 'I know it's Christmas Day,' she said quietly, 'but I want to see Uncle Tim. Don't you *want* me to see him?' She looked at us then, but nobody answered her. 'Anyway,' she went on, 'I haven't far to go to the hospital – what about your poor Granny and your poor aunties having to come all that way to the hospital?'

'They can't be coming here tomorrow!' I protested.

And everybody was protesting again. We were sick and tired of having Granny and the aunties and Uncle Tim's wife and Uncle Tim's neighbours crowding into our kitchen every day for God-knows-how-long. There was always some stranger sitting in the armchair in front of the range, drinking bottles of stout and looking dolefully into the fire and shaking their heads and talking about the will of God. Was it the will of God that we couldn't have Mammy to ourselves in our own kitchen, just for Christmas Day? I said as much to Mammy then, raising my voice to make my protest heard above the indignant din of the others.

She looked at me when silence fell upon our candle-lighted kitchen and she said: 'He's my only brother. I thought you'd understand.'

It was unfair. I had made the weekly visits with her to the Bargain Stores in Shop Street, watching as the thin, dark-haired woman in the shop recorded payments against the toys that would be delivered that night by Santa Claus. I had carried those toys out the Line the previous week, hidden under brown bags of sugar and tea in the shopping-bags, and I had stowed them on top of the wardrobe in my parents' bedroom, safe from inquisitive eyes and searching hands of small brothers and sisters – all this, while strangers hijacked my mother and left our kitchen empty for weeks on end. There was only almond icing on the second Christmas cake: there hadn't even been time enough for Mammy to put the white caster-sugar icing on top of it.

'It's not fair, Mammy!' was all I could say.

Our eyes met above the candle-flame. 'No,' she said, 'it's not fair.' Her level gaze allowed no flinching: there was another kitchen, in another town, which would feel empty that Christmas.

Miriam could see that too. 'Who'll get the Christmas dinner ready for Uncle Tim's kids?' she asked.

'Their Mammy will.'

'Is she not coming tomorrow to see Uncle Tim in the san?'

'She's going to stay at home with the children,' Mammy answered. 'Just your Granny and your aunties will be coming tomorrow.'

'I'll help you with the dinner,' Miriam said. 'The table isn't big enough for everybody to sit down together.'

The hackney driver would have to be given his dinner as well. I wished we had a goose like last year, but Mammy had brought home a pair of chickens from the market beside the Protestant church in town. We'd tried to help her pluck the two birds the night before when she'd come home from the hospital. The sickly naked skin of the birds made me think of Uncle Tim, dying in a hospital bed. I'd never seen a man die, except in the pictures, where heroes whispered death-bed confessions and bad guys gasped final obscenities.

'Can I go out to see Uncle Tim tomorrow?' I asked her.

She shook her head. 'There's no children allowed in,' she said to me. 'Anyway, I'd prefer you to remember him the way he was.' She sat on the armchair beside the fire, still wearing her overcoat. She bent towards the glowing bars, her palms outstretched. Her shoulders sagged. For the first time I noticed the grey strands amid the darkness of her hair. Martha and Danny pushed closer to her, and Mammy straightened in the chair and drew Martha onto her lap. Miriam and Jacky stood on either side of the armchair, touching her as they talked. I watched them for a while, half-listening to the childish talk about Santa Claus and toys and chimneys. I was ashamed of my outburst now, but felt unable to tell her so. I crossed the half-lighted room and stood beside Miriam. Mammy turned her head, as if sensing my presence.

'I'll help with the dinner too,' I said. 'I'll do the washing-up.'

'You're a great boy,' she said to me.

Martha pushed her face against Mammy's. 'Amn't I a great girl?' she shouted.

'You're a great girl altogether!' Mammy said, laughing. Her eyes held mine, and I knew I was forgiven.

Uncle Tim died on St Stephen's Day.

Granny and the aunts and Uncle Tim's widow crowded into the kitchen of Number 2 the day after he died, dressed in black coats, with black scarves on their heads and black shoes on their feet. They drank cups of tea and bottles of stout and filled the kitchen with cigarette smoke. When they crushed the cigarette-ends on top of the range you could see the thick smears of lipstick on the broken butts. Their eyes were red as their mouths.

When it was time to go, Mammy checked the two brown suitcases again, to make sure that we had forgotten nothing. Granny and the aunts and Uncle Tim's widow would travel in the hackney; my father had arranged for a hackney from town to take all of us to Mammy's home-town for the funeral.

My father sat in the front beside the driver. Miriam and Jacky and I pushed alongside Mammy on the back seat, with the two smaller ones perched on our laps. I managed to turn my head and look through the rear window of the car as we drove alongside the Magazine towards the Gate. In the early December afternoon our house looked empty, the front door closed, the windows unlighted. The Suttons' house had looked like that, after the family had gone to Coventry.

We were *en route* to the sanatorium, to drive from there behind the black hearse taking Uncle Tim's remains to the graveyard in the town where he and Mammy had been children together. We'd be away for two days. The night before when Mammy had told us about the funeral journey, it had seemed like an adventure. Now it merely seemed what it was: a journey to bury Mammy's only brother. Her eyes were red and our closed-up home looked like the Suttons'.

We were waved through the main gates of the Barracks by the new PA who knew hardly anybody's name.

TWELVE

'Time up!'

Little Brother Martin's shout from the top of the room signalled the end to the examination, an end to another school day. Even standing on the dais, he would hardly rise above my shoulder. Only for a second I watched him, hauling himself higher on the platform, his small mouth puckered in his small neat face. I bent again over my paper, scribbling furiously to complete the last question of the history examination. I didn't care much about the workings of the Hanseatic League, but I didn't want to do badly in my first examination in the secondary school. Besides, I knew the answer; if I hadn't lost time by being distracted about what was going on at home, I'd have been finished by now.

'I said the time is up!' Brother Martin's shout was louder now. 'Everybody stop writing! Put the pens down!'

I wrote with even greater vigour. Around me, papers rustled, desk lids banged and mathematical sets rattled in their tin boxes. The entire school, from First Year to Sixth Year, was crammed into the enlarged space created by rolling back the partitions that divided the classrooms on the top floor of the school. To prevent copying, or 'cogs' as it was known in the school, you shared a desk with a boy from another year for the four days of the exams. While I hurried feverishly to finish my history paper, I could see from the corner of my eye that the Fifth Year fellow beside me was putting away his maths set after completing his geometry exam.

'Did you not hear me calling "time up"?' Brother Martin was standing beside me. Neatly dressed in his black soutane and a green sash, he looked like a little fellow who was learning to serve Mass.

I stabbed a final full stop on my paper. 'Sorry, Brother,' I said. I might have been scared had it been one of the other Brothers, but everybody knew that Brother Martin was all bark and no bite. He

180

coached the school hurling teams and ran the school bookshop with an easy friendliness that invited familiarity.

Brother Martin grinned at me. When he grinned, his eyes twinkled behind his round glasses. 'Are you finished?' he asked me.

'Yes, Brother.'

'Then be a good man,' he said to me, 'and collect all the history papers for the Second Years.' Inwardly I winced. The idea of parading around the entire floor to collect papers made me blush. I searched for words to beg a reprieve, but none came.

'Hurry up, there's a good lad,' Brother Martin said. He turned on his heel with a swishing of his soutane. There would be no reprieve.

I moved around the floor as quickly as possible. Some of my Second Year classmates chatted and joked as they handed me their answer papers. I ignored the chat and the jokes. Eyes down, face crimson, I darted from desk to desk. I didn't mind too much about the Second Year fellows. It was the guys from the Fifth Year, sharing the desks with our year, who might give me a hard time. I hurried on, praying that I might be left alone. Miraculously, nobody razzed me. I deposited the pile of papers on the teacher's desk with a palpable sense of relief, like a white man who has just run the gauntlet of bloodthirsty Mohicans.

'Are you all right?' Brother Martin was standing on the dais looking strangely at me. 'Is anything wrong?' he asked.

I shook my head and moved smartly back to my desk. How could you tell a teacher that you die a death every time you have to move out of your desk because, although you're the tallest boy in the Second Year, you are also the only fellow still wearing short trousers? The injustice of it all rankled, but I could feel no anger towards my mother. 'I can't get them,' she'd said, when I'd begged her for the longers. 'I just don't have the money.' I no longer complained to her about it, but I took it hard sometimes, being a long-legged thirteen-and-a-half-year-old walking about in short trousers.

The room was emptying rapidly. Voices were raised more loudly than usual, since it was Brother Martin who was in charge. I lingered idly by the desk, trying to drag out the small routine of tidying up my stuff for going home. There wasn't much to gather up after a full day of exams: an Irish history book, a European history book, foolscap writing-paper and a ruler. You brought with you only those books you needed for some last-minute revision. I tied the two books together with my strap, the left-over sheets of foolscap folded between them, and moved reluctantly towards the door.

'Good luck now.' Brother Martin's voice echoed in the now empty exam hall. He was organising the various bundles of answers for the different classes.

'G'bye, Brother,' I called out.

He smiled at me, and bent again to his task of sorting bundles of papers. Through the tall, bare windows behind him you could see the street-lamps of the town shining their pale white light in the darkening evening. The leafless trees in front of the Protestant chapel next door to our school bent in the November wind.

I had been slower than I realised: the school was deserted as I made my way downstairs. The bare wooden stairs creaked eerily in the silence. I passed the school bookshop on the first landing, where Brother Martin sold new and second-hand books for a couple of brief periods each day, before school and during lunch-hour. When I'd gone back to him after a week in the school to trade in my barely-used First Year books for a complete set of Second Year books, he had seemed to grasp at once my difficulty. 'Never mind about your name on these books,' he'd said, gathering up my First Year books from the narrow counter. 'It's not your fault that you got promoted, is it?' I remembered now, as if it were lost forever, his smiling cheerful face when he'd put down the armload of replacement books on the counter and waved away my inquiries about additional cost, his hand raised, palm outward, like a policeman on traffic duty. 'Nothing extra at all to pay,' he'd said, 'sure why would there be?' I'd paid in other ways, sitting among strangers in class, Tommy and Art and Paul lost to me in that other world of First Year.

And now this new development at home. Another familiar world lost. More strangers crowding at my elbow.

I took my overcoat from the racks of coat hangers in the back hall of the school. Somebody had gone home without his coat: a single rubber raincoat dangled from a hook on the bottom row, trailing its tail on the dark red tiles of the hall.

The wind hit me as I crossed the schoolyard to the gym. The vernacular of the secondary school, so confusing at first, was familiar now. Our gym shared nothing with the gymnasium where the soldiers trained; our gym was a long shed where we stored our bicycles. There were other varieties of the unfamiliar to learn, to become accustomed to, to deal in without fear. There was the language of Latin and the gobbledy-gook of Commerce, the notion of different teachers for different subjects, the idea of mid-term exams, such as the one I had just finished. In six or seven weeks' time, as my first term at secondary school came to a close, there would be Christmas exams.

I wheeled my bicycle out of the gym into the yard.

The headmaster seemed to materialise beside me out of the shadows. 'How did you get on in the exams?' he asked.

'Okay,' I said. I wasn't sure how I felt about Brother Francis. It had been his idea to have me moved up a class into Second Year.

He fell into step alongside me as I walked my bike towards the gates. It was an offence to ride your bike across the schoolyard: the punishment varied, depending upon who caught you, from a ticking-off to a couple of slogs. 'Slogs' was also part of the new vernacular – at primary school the teacher administered 'slaps' with the cane.

'Are you getting on okay in Second Year?' Brother Francis asked.

The change of class meant extra work in nearly everything, especially in Latin and mathematics, but he knew that anyway: he'd warned me about it when he told me he was moving me up. 'I think so,' I said.

The headmaster jangled his ring of school keys as we walked. The keys were attached to a little leather purse, like the one Mammy kept her money in. She'd asked me to hurry home to help her. The move would be a big job, she'd told me, and she could do with my help. 'You're late going home this evening,' Brother Francis said. I could hear the query in his voice. I said nothing. We were standing at the gates of the school now. Inadvertently I triggered the bell of my bike and I jumped nervously when it jangled. 'What kept you so late at school?' Brother Francis asked quietly. His face looked kind in the pale light of the street lamp.

'We're moving,' I blurted out. 'We're leaving the Barracks.' My words were bayonets turned upon myself in the sharp evening air.

'Where are you moving to?' the headmaster asked. 'Are you getting a house in the town?'

I shook my head. 'It's just outside the Barracks,' I said, 'down by the railway line.'

'Well, that's not so bad then,' Brother Francis said cheerfully. 'You won't have so far to move.'

Not so far, and yet so very far. A two-storey house set back from the railroad, a stone's throw from the Barracks wall. 'I suppose so,' I said, half-heartedly. It was another world, on the wrong side of the Barracks wall.

'And when are ye moving?' I heard him ask me.

'Today, Brother,' I said. 'They're moving today – I didn't go home for my dinner today because they were moving.' I'd eaten sandwiches and drunk milk in the gym. I'd tasted nothing. The grey army truck was parked in the lee of the Magazine as young recruits carried the beds and glass case and the wardrobes and the other stuff out from Number 2 and arranged it in the back of the lorry while my father gave instructions and I chewed on the tasteless sandwiches in the school gym.

Brother Francis's words brought me back to the evening and the darkness deepening over the empty yard of the school. 'You should be going home,' he was saying. 'I'm sure your mother could do with your help in the new house.'

'I'll be off so,' I said.

'Good luck in the new house,' he said. 'And don't worry, you'll get to like it after a while.' His keys jangled again as he moved towards his house across the road.

I mulled over the headmaster's words as I cycled along the narrow street which was dominated by our school. I had lived with the knowledge of our move for weeks past, and could only move from feelings of regret to anger and back again. Why did we have to move at all, I'd demanded of my mother, and I'd shot all her explanations down with scorn and argument and even tears. Wasn't Number 2 'a house of our own'? And weren't all my friends in the Quarters? And why did we have to have a garden anyway – we could grow potatoes in the plots like the other soldiers did, couldn't we?

'You'll be glad of it later on,' she said, 'when you're older.' Adults always thought they knew best. You were over thirteen years old and they were still telling you what you should be doing and what you ought to be thinking. It just wasn't fair.

I cycled across O'Brien's Bridge and on up into Shop Street. I had no lamp on my bike and I kept an eye out for the big guard who'd given me a lecture the previous week on the illegality of riding a bicycle after sunset without a lamp. No excuses the next time, he'd said, collecting books from the library or not. There was no sign of him on the street. The shop windows were lighted, but I paid them no attention, not even to the books on display at O'Gorman's. A few of the Fifth Year fellows were hanging around the door of the Marian Café, talking to a couple of girls from the Mercy. You could tell by their navy-blue uniforms that they were at the Mercy. I stared straight ahead as I rode past, terrified lest my short trousers became the target of derisory wolf-whistles and jeers. I knew that the older fellows drank coffee in the Marian. I wondered what it would be like, sitting at a table while a waitress brought you coffee and you talked to girls. You'd have to have long trousers to go in there and you'd have to have money to pay for the coffee, and maybe I'd hate the taste of coffee . . .

Dublin-time on Dillon's clock said five to five. It was later than I realised. I pedalled harder, up the incline towards the Square. Maybe all the moving was finished by now. Suppose they'd forgotten my two boxes of books and the new people had already moved into Number 2 and torn and messed up my books? I swung round by the black railings of the Square. The dark road was slick with rain-washed cowdung after the cattle fair of the morning. The wet dung shone under the yellow light that spilled down from the glass doors of the railway hotel.

I pushed up the station slope, past the parked buses, and I remembered that first journey to school with Mammy, and how I had drawn closer to her in the shadow of these grey buildings. The sweat was cold on my back now, as I bent over the handlebars, forcing the bicycle up the steepness of the Bandroom hill. I freewheeled down the far side: before me the Line twisted like a grey snake through the darkness, past the McCormacks' house and on across the three bridges, up to the little chapel and the Barracks.

The arched windows in the grey stone chapel were dark: in a little while the PA would send a private soldier out from the Gate to switch on the Chapel lights. For now, however, the little building was a slab of darkness in the unfriendly gloom.

Bartley was on duty at the Gate. He was standing beside the pot-bellied stove when I pushed in the door, his thumbs hooked into the breast pockets of his tunic. His pistol-holster rode high on his left hip, the handle of the weapon facing across his midriff. When I'd been younger I had pondered the merits of this holster position as compared with the classic Wild West slot, the gun slung low on the right thigh to facilitate a quick draw. These days, the Subjective Mood of Latin verbs seemed more relevant to my daily work than Bartley's slickness on the draw.

I felt his eyes boring into me from behind the thick lenses of his spectacles. 'Where d'*you* think you're going?' he demanded.

'Home,' I said.

Bartley unhooked his right hand from his tunic and gestured backwards over his shoulder with his thumb. 'Down there,' he said, 'not in here.'

'But – '

'Your Mammy carried the last boxload of your stuff out through this Gate not half an hour ago,' Bartley interrupted me. 'She told me herself it was the last boxload – in fact, she told me it was a load of your own books that were in the box.' His words hit me in the pit of my stomach. I was unable to move, transfixed half-in and half-out in the doorway of the Gate. 'Wouldn't you think you'd have got home a bit early today to give your Mammy a hand with the movin' an' all?' Bartley added.

'I had an exam,' I said lamely.

Barley snorted. 'The other lads had exams too,' he said, 'but they came through here a good half an hour ago.'

I looked at Bartley, his great bulk straining against the confines of his uniform, and sensed instinctively a change in his attitude towards me. The familiarity of years, the mock-seriousness with which he had so often threatened to incarcerate my pals and myself in the guardroom – all that shared intimacy seemed gone, and not just because I was no longer a kid who rode the Oregon Trail with Kit Carson.

I said nothing, for there was nothing more to be said.

I backed my bicycle out of the doorway and let the heavy door swing shut behind me. I turned my eyes from the dark-green stretch of lawn in front of the Officers' Mess and, beyond it, the grey expanse of the parade ground, and I swung my leg over the bicycle, heading for my new home.

186

In the shelter of the high Barracks wall there was no wind, and the tyres crunched noisily on the gravelled road. I tried to shut out from my mind everything that lay on the other side of the wall, but to no avail: I thought I heard Art calling to me before he turned the gable of the Married Quarters to go into Number 1, but it was only the wind whistling through the barbed wire of the turfyard.

I had passed beyond the corner of the Barracks wall by now. I stopped, leaning on the handlebars of the bicycle. Below me, at the foot of a steep slope, lay the small terrace of three houses. The house at the furthest end of the terrace was ours. Like the other houses, it was two storeys high, with grey plastered walls and red bricks around the windows and the front door. Each house had its own garden, surrounded by tall hedges. There were young people of my own age in these houses, but I knew them only to see. Their fathers were also in the army, for these too were army homes, but they kept to themselves. Sometimes, when I passed by these garden walls, they might look up and say hello, but more often than not they ignored you and carried on cutting their lawns or trimming their hedges.

The windows in all three houses were lighted. Even as I watched, the front door of the furthest house swung open, and I saw my mother standing there, framed in the rectangle of yellow light. She couldn't see me, leaning on my bicycle in the darkness at the top of the hill, but I knew from the way she turned her face upwards that she was waiting for me, searching the darkness. And she'd want to know how the exams had gone: sometimes her fierce pride in my school progress made me blush, especially when announced with such delight to the neighbours. She turned her head as if someone had called her indoors, and in a moment I saw my sister Miriam come and stand in the doorway beside my mother. I saw my mother smile, and she reached down to hold Miriam's hand. They were smiling in the lighted doorway as I freewheeled downhill towards home.

EPILOGUE

Nobody lives in the Barracks anymore. Some years back they turned the Married Quarters into offices.

I have never seen these offices. I never will. There may be a computer humming electronically now in Number 2, or a fax machine spewing forth memoranda from some distant United Nations outpost, but in my mind's eye there is forever that big kitchen and my mother at work, always at work, stooping to remove yet another cake or tart from the oven, or black-leading the range, or knitting yet another jumper or cardigan even while she took her rare rest in the army armchair. Phones may well ring now in Number 2, and photocopiers may clatter, but in my heart Number 2 rings only with the competing war cries of my brothers and sisters and, in the background, the clipped tones of a BBC announcer reading the racing results from Epsom or Newbury . . .

As with childhood gangs everywhere, our gang also is scattered. Art, who survived a hundred shared and savage skirmishes with Indians and rustlers, teaches English in a remote and gentle backwater in the north-west: on the rare occasions when we meet, I never remember to ask him if he ever refers his students to the rich pickings of the old comics of the Wild West. Paul, whose only-child status made him visibly softer than the rest of us but spiced our vocabulary with American gangsterisms picked up from AFN on the wireless, went to teach in a tough school in a tough Dublin district. Bobby joined the army at a young age, retired on full pension – also at an early age – and went to work in a local bank. We meet and chat frequently in the bank, sometimes about the difficulties of fatherhood. Tommy, the son of the Barracks barber, worked as an accountant in London before returning to settle in Dublin. We have never been together as a group since we finished secondary school.

Our town has changed, pushing itself ever outwards, building in all directions except on the sea. The wide-open spaces around the Barracks are covered in vast housing estates: the new settlers have fenced in the plains of our Wild West with a mortgaged fervour.

The Line is the same, a ribbon of path linking town and Barracks as it always did. And yet it is not the same: the Furze on both sides is no longer the mysterious spaces of Wyoming and Montana, but yet more acres of houses and roads. The cross of stones on the grass below Paddy Walsh's bridge has disappeared under the tarred surface of one of these roads.

Above all, the Barracks itself has changed: that unique world of military men and heroic women has disappeared forever. And heroic these mothers truly were – in the midst of a male hierarchy they sustained themselves, their families and one another with a modicum of material wealth and an abundance of courage and love.

When my father retired from the army in the late '70s, he did so as sergeant-major, the highest rank that can be obtained by an NCO. The Barracks honoured his lifetime of service with a guard of honour: flags flew and a bugler blew. A few years previously, while driving him south to Kilkenny to visit his people, I had asked my father why he had joined the army. I had expected the explanation of unemployment, the solution of food, shelter and clothing. The answer was different: 'There was a war coming, and I wanted to serve my country.' It was an answer that had been given without self-consciousness, with no attempt at the posture of heroics. His words came back to me on the last official day of his career: you could not doubt the esteem and respect in which he was held by his army colleagues, of all ranks, as if they too had recognised the generosity of his commitment to the service and the unyielding integrity of his life. Ghosts from Spion Kop and Gallipoli marched past on that last afternoon, and a bugle-note echoed from the Little Big Horn, as my father took the salute.

By then Mammy was dead. Her remains lay in the New Cemetery, not far from the spooky caretaker's lodge which had been the home of the unenvied brother and sister who boarded our school bus in the mornings. The grave held only her poor, cancer-withered body. Her indomitable spirit, and that of the Barracks, lived on in my heart.

Mine is not the only heart, I suspect, in which it lives on.